Other Books by Tom Julien

"Four Laws for Effective Communicators," (booklet), BMH Books

Inherited Wealth, Studies in Ephesians, BMH Books

Seize the Moment, Stories of an Awesome God Empowering Ordinary People,
Grace Brethren International Missions

Spiritual Greatness, Studies in Exodus, BMH Books

What Others Are Saying...

"This book is an appeal to disciples everywhere for the church to be reunited with her mission. As a child both of the church and of missions, Tom Julien writes with authority and passion from the platform of a long and fruitful ministry. I heartily commend this book to you for Christ and His Kingdom."

> Luis Bush
> Former Director, AD 2000 and Beyond
> International Facilitator, Transform World Connections

"This book must be read. I have spoken at hundreds of churches that have left the old paradigm, and now operate in a more Acts 13 biblical way. I hope this book will help you and your church to make the change."

> George Verwer
> Founder, Operation Mobilization

"In spite of the fact that most church leaders see The Great Commission as the marching orders for the church, they treat it as one of their programs instead of the fundamental purpose of the church. *Antioch Revisited* will help your church become a base, not a basin; a sending agency rather than a collection agency."

> David Mays
> Great Lakes Regional Director
> Advancing Churches in Missions Commitment (ACMC)

"In our highly individualistic society it might be expected that we would divide the church and her mission into compartments better managed by separate staff, having separate budgets and emphasized by separate programs. Tom Julien's book effectively helps us put the pieces back together as they were in the beginning in the book of Acts. *Antioch Revisited* is a must read in a day when cultural forms have led the way and biblical forms have been left behind."

> Tom Stallter
> Professor of Intercultural Studies
> Grace College and Theological Seminary

"Tom Julien has mentored a generation of pastors and missionaries in the critical importance of reuniting the church with her mission. I'm excited that his insights are now captured in an engaging manner that will impact many more who long to see the church fulfill her mission in the world."

> Dave Guiles
> Executive Director
> Grace Brethren International Missions

DEDICATION

To those churches that are more concerned

about their sending capacity than their seating capacity

Contents

About this book...

It is one of the great tragedies of church history—the divorce between the church and her mission. Today few churches even know that the divorce occurred, making it even more painful. The separation has persisted so long that it seems normal.

The divorce occurred early, when churches gradually ceased functioning as God's embassies in a world which was not their own and began pursuing their own interests. It continued through the centuries, during which their mission was relegated to various kinds of specialized agencies. It continues today, causing us to see mission as something grafted onto the church, rather than growing out of it.

Antioch Rekindled is the account of someone who worked his way out of this dichotomy, discovering that mission is woven into the very essence of the church. Though John the missionary is a fictional character, his story could well be my own. His youthful years in his church are similar to my own, as are his experiences at university and later with his missionary agency. It was only after many years as a missionary that I, like John, fully understood that the church is missionary by nature, that the Great Commission is the fundamental law of her existence, and that the Spirit of the church and of mission are one and the same.

For me the process began with a book called *Pentecost and Missions*, by Harry Boer, a book long since out of print. I had the good fortune to come across this book early in my missionary career, and during the years that followed, the concepts that were planted by Boer germinated. Here is a typical quote from Boer:

> One hardly knows where in Acts to look for a distinction between Church and missions. Restlessly the Spirit

> drives the Church to witness, and continually churches rise out of the witness. The Church is missionary Church. She is not missionary Church in the sense that she is 'very much interested' in missions, or that she 'does a great deal' for missions. In Acts missions is not a hobby of the 'evangelical section' of the Church. The Church as a whole is missionary in all her relationships. (Harry R. Boer, *Pentecost and Missions, 1979* Eerdmans, pp 161-162)

In the early 1980s these concepts were the basis of some intense discussions in the Europe team of Grace Brethren International Missions, the mission in which my wife and I served. Several of us had begun to feel personally the consequences of the divorce. We wanted our churches to get a sense of the significance of the times and to be a part of the network of churches that God was choosing throughout the world to be a part of His global team. It was not that our churches were uninterested in missions. For most of them, however, missions focused on what the church did *for* the missionary, more so than *through* the missionary.

As we worked through these concepts in our own family of churches, we soon learned that we were not alone in our pilgrimage. The last few decades have witnessed a growing and widespread awareness of the need for bringing back together what God never meant to be separated—the church and her mission. Other books have taken the place of Boer's *Pentecost and Mission,* such as *God's Missionary People* by Charles Van Engen and Patrick Johnstone's *The Church is Bigger Than You Think*, indispensable reading for every pastor, missionary, and seminary professor. The impact of such organizations as ACMC (Advancing Churches in Missions Commitment) has been considerable. Literally hundreds of local churches from all denominations have become models of what can happen when the church moves out of the maintenance mode and into the mission mode.

If you are a part of one of those churches, a church that has become proactive with respect to the Great Commission, you probably do not have to read further. But if the church and mission still occupy two distinct compartments of your brain, read on. John's discoveries have the potential of triggering a personal revolution in your thinking, pushing you to a level of spiritual significance that you have not yet experienced.

And if you are among those who choose to read on, let me give you a suggestion. Don't try to be too analytical. *Antioch Rekindled* presents a process that could be of great help to your church or ministry, but forget about trying to duplicate what happened in John's life and church.

Instead, just settle back and let John lead you through his journey. When you encounter a concept that makes sense, an idea that jumps out at you, stop and write it down, so that you can come back and think it through in the context of your own situation. These concepts will become seed truths that have the potential of germinating and producing fruit in your life and church. If the entire story plants only one seed truth, it will be well worth the few hours that it will take to read through the book.

If you choose to go further, seeking to implement these concepts into your church in a more systematic way, a study manual has been included as the second part of the book. This manual has been used as a basis for mission seminars and study conferences in dozens of churches, as well as seminary courses. It might prove to be a helpful tool for you as you seek to share John's discoveries with others.

Antioch Rekindled is not for missiologists, already knowledgeable in all these areas, but for the ordinary people whom God has called into the kingdom for such a time as this. When ordinary people begin to see their extraordinary potential, life is no longer a trivial pursuit.

Tom Julien
Winona Lake, Indiana
June 2006

John's Story

Chapter One

HILLSIDE'S WAKE-UP CALL

It was not the usual Sunday morning at Hillside Community Church. Many of the people felt an uncommon sense of anticipation as they found their seats. John, their very own missionary, had just flown in from Africa two days before. Children kept looking back at the door, hoping to be the first to see him walk in, wondering whether he would be wearing a colorful African costume. John's stories kept them on the edge of their seats—not always the case with Pastor Smith's sermons.

John was weary and somewhat confused. He had hardly slept on the plane Thursday night flying into Europe. Now, after crossing the Atlantic, he was experiencing jet lag. Saturday had been a family day. Though delightful, it had been draining. His only contact with the pastor had been a brief phone call.

He knew these conditions were not ideal for renewing contact with his home church. A lot had happened in his life and thinking during the weeks before he left Africa. He had suggested to Pastor Smith that his speaking engagement be postponed until the following week so that he and the pastor could spend some time together. "Can you imagine how the people would feel if you were there and they could not hear from you?" the pastor exclaimed. "We're going to take advantage of listening to you as often as we can."

Ever since John had become a missionary he was something of a local hero, especially among the children of the church. This did not necessarily mean that the people felt any personal involvement in John's ministry, or even a sense of obligation to the Great Commission. For them, missions was identified with John himself. They were proud of him, and some of them looked upon him almost with a sense of awe. He was "*their* missionary." Few in the church, however, had the slightest idea that what John was doing was "*their* ministry." Their role was clear—it was to send the monthly check to the mission agency, and they were doing it faithfully.

But now *their* missionary was struggling with his thoughts. Only he knew how radically his thinking had been impacted by new insights he had experienced during the previous month. What would he say when he walked up to the pulpit? They would want stories, the kind he usually told. He knew it would have to be different.

> I need to talk about a problem that exists in the church. That problem is divorce. I am referring to a divorce between the church and her mission.

John walked into the church building, shaking hands with friends as he moved toward a front pew. Most eyes were glued on him during the opening part of the service. He seemed to be more serious than they had remembered. When he stepped up to speak, the people sensed urgency in his voice.

This is what he said.

"I have looked forward to this morning for a long time. You are my home church. This is where I grew up. This is where I first heard the Word of God. In a sense you are my spiritual family, even though this morning I am meeting some of you for the first time. Though my life is quite different from yours, I know you are interested in me. Thanks for your expressions of that interest, such as the cards you sent me on my birthday. I hope that while I am home I will be able to spend some time with you who would like to know more than I will be able to share today.

"But today I want to use this time to do something different. I have a burden to share with you. I hope you will not be disappointed if I do not say much this morning about my life in Africa—that will have to come a little later.

"I do not want to offend anyone, but I feel that I need to talk about a problem that exists in the church. *That problem is divorce.*"

At those words the people became tense. Several of the couples began to look at each other nervously. The pastor stiffened and stared at John, wondering what would come next. John continued.

"Please do not think that my words refer to the personal life of anyone here. I am not speaking about divorce with respect to couples. The divorce I am referring to is far more serious. It is a divorce within the church itself—not just our church, but the church as a whole.

"I am referring to a divorce between the church and her mission. Let me try to explain.

"If you look into the gospel of Matthew you will read about two encounters Jesus had with His disciples—encounters that have enormous implications for our lives. The first is what I call the Great Prediction. It's the encounter where Jesus says He will build His church. The second encounter took place several months later, when Jesus gave His disciples the Great Commission."

John related how these two encounters represent two streams that came together on the day of Pentecost to form a mighty river. It was then, when the Holy Spirit fell upon the disciples who were praying in the upper room, that the Great Prediction was fulfilled, for the church was born. John told them how, from then on, the Apostles wove together the church and mission into the fabric of their ministries to such an extent that you can see the church only through the Great Commission, and you can see the Great Commission only through the church.

"You see, at the day of Pentecost it was as if there was a marriage—a marriage between the church and her mission. But tragically this beautiful marriage ended in divorce.

"This divorce does not affect our church alone. It concerns

thousands of churches all over the world. The divorce occurred very early in the history of the church as a whole, when the church became more interested in establishing an earthly kingdom than bringing the good news to those who had never heard. It continued through the centuries, as missions became the responsibility of specialized agencies rather than churches. And it exists today where missions consists mainly of budgeting money to support missionaries rather than making disciples of all nations, starting right where we live.

"Dear friends, we have all suffered the consequences of this divorce. You and I are its children. You have suffered, perhaps without being aware of it, because this divorce has in many ways impoverished the church spiritually. But I want you to know that we missionaries have also suffered. Sometimes we feel a little bit like spiritual orphans. We enjoy our visitation rights. It is wonderful to be here. We are able to serve only because of your financial support. But we do not want that support to be like alimony. We would like to feel that we are a real part of a family. We would like to feel that what we are doing is really *your* ministry, something that you are doing *through* us.

"I feel like I am a child both of the church and of missions. Yet sometimes I wonder where I really belong. I sure would like to see my spiritual parents bought back together.

"I want to see the church reunited with her mission."

Chapter Two

THE CALL

Conversation was difficult after that Sunday morning service at Hillside Community Church. Most of the people had no idea what John was trying to say. Pastor Smith simply stated, "John, we have to talk." John's parents, who had looked forward so eagerly to his visit, seemed confused, but they did not feel the freedom to express their feelings at the dinner table.

What had changed John?

To answer that question we first need to learn more about Hillside Community Church. Then we will have to live through John's final weeks in Africa to discover how his thinking had been impacted. All this will require several chapters of reading before we will be able to come back to pick up the story, learning what happened at Hillside after John's message.

Hillside Community was a fairly typical Bible church in a small Midwestern city. It had started as a split from an older, more traditional church in the community because of the liberal trends in the denomination. The new church experienced some exciting years, but soon some of the families began having difficulty submitting to the leadership of the pastors. The spirit of independence created by the division sowed seeds that continued to trouble relationships.

John, with a natural sensitivity to spiritual things, would quickly attach himself to each new pastor. After a few years, however, a rift would develop between the pastor and several of the leading families of the church, eventually resulting in the departure of the minister. Because these situations were accompanied by harmful criticism of the pastor, they hurt John deeply.

All this had a profound influence on his view of the church.

As a young person finishing high school, John was convinced he wanted to give his life to God in ministry but was not sure what steps to take next. He had committed his life to God and received encouragement from many people. Yet he had never received any specific guidance nor had much experience in ministry. He could never remember leading anyone to Christ personally. The only advice he was given was to attend a Christian college, which he gladly followed.

His college experience was almost uniformly positive. He found friends who had a true desire to make their lives count for God. Further, the type of relationship he would like to have achieved with pastors in his church became a reality with a few of his professors. He admired them and they became spiritual counselors as well as teachers.

> Pastors ...were supportive of his ministry, but often embarrassed that they could do nothing personally to help. He realized that it was his ministry, not theirs.

It was at a large nondenominational missions conference that John had his first experience with missions. His most overwhelming impression of that conference was the considerable number of mission organizations that were represented and the great diversity of their ministries. After browsing through the displays and reading some of the literature, John concluded that nearly every imaginable profession could be exercised on the mission field.

At an evening rally, John joined hundreds of others in making a formal commitment of his life to missions. The appeal from a veteran missionary was powerful, moving many in the audience to tears. "How could anybody sit still in a world where the needs are so great?" reflected John in the months following. His commitment was profound and would affect the rest of his life.

In the months that followed, John began to pursue opportunities available in the various mission agencies he had encountered. After much prayer he finally focused on the one he thought fit best.

Until now John had had no contact with his church about these decisions, nor had he felt it was necessary, for he talked freely with many of his friends at college as well as several of the professors. They were very supportive and gave him valuable counsel.

John was impressed by the mission agency he had chosen. It was efficient and businesslike in its response to his inquiries. Further, the men he eventually met were genuine men of God, the kind of people he could admire and in whom he could put confidence. As he went through the long process of testing and orientation, he felt that no stone was left unturned. He could leave for the field with a conviction in his heart that he was doing the right thing and with assurance that, humanly speaking, he could adequately do the job he was expected to do.

Though his church played almost no role in John's decision to become a missionary, news of the decision brought them a feeling of pleasure. He was the first young person in the church to offer his life for full-time ministry. Until John made his decision the church had never become involved in any missionary activity outside the local community. But the letter from the mission agency requesting their recommendation produced excitement. When the pastor approached the board to request that John be put on the budget, nearly all responded favorably. As was expected, some of the people expressed concern about giving money to the "foreign field" when there were so many needs at home and the congregation was struggling to meet its local budget. Yet the support amount proposed by the board was modest, and when it was presented to the people it was accepted with enthusiasm.

About this time John began a period that eventually lasted two years—one he would have liked to forget. In order to get to the field he had to raise financial support. This was his first genuine contact with churches other than his own. As he would look back on this experience in later years, it would almost always be associated with negative feelings. It was not that anyone was unkind with him; in fact, almost everyone he met was basically encouraging.

It was just that he did not seem to belong anywhere. Pastors with whom he had spoken were supportive of his ministry, but often embarrassed that they could do nothing personally to help. He realized that it was his ministry, not theirs. He realized too that they saw him essentially as someone needing financial support rather than one who was a part of the ministry of their church. Nothing he said seemed to change this situation.

It seemed that he traveled thousands of miles during those two years. It seemed also that he experienced the whole gamut of emotions, from excitement to borderline depression. He prayed a great deal and tried to perfect his presentation dozens of times, even occasionally resorting to telling people that he was not interested in their financial commitment but wanted only their prayers. He did this with a tinge of guilt, wondering in his heart if he was faithfully representing his true feelings.

Gradually some churches did respond. Further, he found open doors in the lives of many of the friends he had made in college, who in turn introduced him to other new friends motivated by concern for reaching the world. These were mainly businessmen, some of whom were dedicating much of their income to getting the gospel out. Few of them, however, saw any vital connection between their giving and the ministry of their churches. They usually made their choices on the basis of how well they knew the people they were supporting.

John finally arrived in Africa, a fully supported missionary. He adjusted well to his new environment and after several years could look back with satisfaction on a life that was both rich and productive. He thanked God that He was indeed at work in the hearts and lives of His people. The Bible Institute in which he was teaching impacted many people. His own experience in college had given him excellent role models that he sought to emulate, and he was consciously trying to groom his best students for a formal teaching ministry—the ministry he enjoyed so much.

Chapter Three

THE DISCOVERY

Teaching at the Bible Institute in Africa had become a comfortable life for John. He settled into a routine that he enjoyed, one he anticipated would continue for years to come.

Then something happened, something that began a process that would transform his vision of the church and her mission.

He was teaching through the book of Acts, as he had done many times. The day came for him to discuss the first few verses of Acts 13, an account of one of the significant occurrences in the history of the early church.

The setting was the church of Antioch, where believers were first called Christians. Among those God had called together in that church were a number of outstanding men whom the Lord had sent as prophets and teachers.

As the believers of the church worshiped God and fasted, the Holy Spirit said, "Set apart for me Barnabas and Saul for the work to which I have called them" (Acts 13:2). The believers continued to fast and pray, doubtless in an attitude of deep soul-searching. Then in obedience to the call of the Spirit of the Lord, they laid their hands upon those two men, a sign both of their recognition of God's anointing and of their responsibility as a church. They released Barnabas and Saul as missionaries, sent by the Lord to pioneer what would be the most significant missionary outreach in the history of the church.

As John taught through those first three verses he tried to paint a visual picture of just what happened on that significant day. In his previous classes he had taught this incident merely as a historic event in the early church. Now he was trying to put himself in their situation and experience what they were living—to understand it from the inside out. In doing so he began to sense that the same Spirit who had sent those first apostles was trying to break into his own heart. As he continued to reflect, he felt a growing conviction that the Antioch experience was far more than a glimpse into history. It was a divinely inspired model of how the church ought to function.

> In the church of Antioch, missions grew out of the local church, rather than being grafted onto it.

What he saw seemed so obvious that he could not believe he had missed it in his previous studies. In the church of Antioch, missions *grew out* of the local church, *rather than being grafted onto* it. Though obvious, this was something so different from his own experience that it was almost like entering a new world. If the Antioch church was supposed to be an example, modern missions somehow had lost the blueprint.

These first missionaries received their call *in their church*, not in a missions conference. The call came through *prayer*, not persuasion. The Antioch church claimed responsibility for mission by laying hands upon the missionaries before releasing them. That meant much more than writing a check for financial support. For the church at Antioch there was no divorce between the church and her mission in the world.

Gradually John began to understand some of his own struggles as a missionary—the spiritual loneliness that resulted from his having so few real roots in his church. He thought of how little influence his church had on his own call and training for missions. He remembered the distress of the nearly two years spent visiting one church after another trying to raise financial support, realizing that he was coming to them almost as a charity—but that he was someone who did not really belong to them. He realized that he considered what he was doing in Africa to be *his* ministry, not an extension of the ministry of his church.

As the scales began to fall from his eyes he did not realize how far-reaching the consequences would be.

Though John tried to convey some of these thoughts to his students when he arrived in class that morning, he knew he was not making much sense. When he left class he was glad he did not have responsibilities during the weekend. He knew the missionary guesthouse in the nearby city would afford him some privacy. He threw some things together and took off.

At first it was hard to concentrate. Too many thoughts were fighting for his attention. Gradually, however, his thinking began to focus on those two significant encounters of Jesus with His disciples recorded in Matthew's gospel, the encounters John would later share on that fateful morning in Hillside Community Church.

John reflected on the encounter recorded in Matthew 16:18-19, where Jesus stated: "I will build my church." As he pondered the meaning of the word Jesus used for the church, *ekklesia* (a body of *called* out ones), he realized that the *call* was foundational to the very existence of the church. The church would have to continue to call or else she would cease to exist as the true body of Christ. She would simply become an ecclesiastical institution.

Church…called out ones. John had always heard that the church was missionary by what she did to promote missions. He was beginning to see that the church is missionary not primarily by what she *does,* but by what she *is*—that the church is missionary by her very *nature,* not merely by her activities. Mission is an expression of her *essence*. It is encoded into her DNA.

He focused on another encounter of Jesus and His disciples, this one on a mountain in Galilee. It was the encounter that provided the setting for the Great Commission recorded in Matthew 28:18-20.

As John reflected on the Great Commission in light of Jesus' prediction of the church, it began to dawn on him that the Great

Commission was essentially the *expression* of what Jesus had said in *essence* when He met with His disciples in Caesarea Philippi.

For the first time in his life John understood that the Great Commission is not an external commandment imposed upon the church, but a statement of the life principle of the church. It is the fundamental law of the very existence of the church, for it is the expression of her essence.

> For the first time in his life John understood that the Great Commission is... the fundamental law of the very existence of the church, for it is the expression of her essence.

"If the disciples had really understood what Jesus said in Matthew 16, they would have been able to write the Great Commission themselves." John began to realize that the Great Commission was not just for those who are missionary-minded; it is given to the church as a whole. It was given by the Lord of the church, to the foundation stones of the church, as an expression of the church's earthly purpose.

"Things are becoming more clear," thought John, as he struggled to process these concepts. He saw Matthew 16 and 28 as two strands in God's cosmic plan that were fused together on the day of Pentecost.

Why was there no dichotomy between the church and mission at Antioch? It was because at Pentecost there had been an *organic union* between the two. Things that are joined *organizationally* can be separated without damage. But *organic* unions grow out of life, and with respect to the church, this life has its source in the Spirit of Christ Himself.

"*The Spirit of Christ is the Spirit of the church,*" he reminded himself. No need to prove that. We were all baptized by one Spirit into one body, as Paul said in 1 Corinthians 12:13.

"*The Spirit of Christ is the Spirit of mission.*" God's Spirit is the *paraklete*—the One who does the calling. He is not merely a comforter who is called to come alongside the believer; He is the advocate who comes alongside to call. He is the one who convicts the world with respect to sin, righteousness, and judgment. "You will receive power when the Holy Spirit comes on you; and you will be my *witnesses*" (Acts 1:8, emphasis added).

There is only one Spirit. John almost laughed at how obvious this was; then he began to reflect on the profound truth he had deduced. *If indeed the Spirit of Christ is both the Spirit of the church and the Spirit of mission, and if indeed there is but one Spirit, then to grieve or quench the Spirit of mission is to grieve or quench the Spirit of the church, for this is the only Spirit that exists. This means quenching the Spirit of love, joy, peace, patience, kindness, goodness, faithfulness, gentleness, and self-control.*

"No wonder so many churches are having problems," thought John, as he reflected upon the churches that supported him. "It all seems so obvious," he thought. "Why have I not seen these things before? Why do we not see more churches having the same experience as the church of Antioch? Why do there seem to be two compartments in my brain—one for the church and another for mission? Why are missionary conferences often so exotic that most people can hardly identify with the Great Commission? What has gone wrong?"

Then the sad truth began to dawn upon him, the truth that would later create so much uneasiness among the people at Hillside Community. At Pentecost there had been a marriage between the church and her mission. But a divorce had occurred—a terrible divorce with ruinous consequences both for the church and her mission.

It was then, too, that John first realized he was a child of this divorce.

⤞Chapter Four⤝

A NEW WAY OF SEEING

In the days that followed, John seemed to be living in two worlds—the familiar one he had always known, and the exciting new world he was discovering. As he finished his courses and prepared his students for their exams, he wondered whether his teaching was really penetrating their lives. He was *transplanting* biblical knowledge but was he really *planting* the biblical concepts that would change their values and give them a new worldview? So much of what he was trying to teach had never really been personalized in his own life. His students could repeat back to him the things he shared, yet were these truths really being planted deeply enough to germinate and produce fruit?

This new world was becoming more and more real. It was not enough merely to *know* what members of the early church did. John was learning that their experiences provided principles that needed to be lived out in our own lives.

He felt he was alone in his struggles. When his coworkers remarked that he seemed preoccupied, he replied that he was thinking through some pretty deep issues. He knew some of them were concerned that he was wrestling with personal problems, but he chose not to share until his thoughts could ripen.

The school year would soon end and he would have to prepare for his departure. John knew he had to talk with others. Since coming to Africa he had formed deep relationships with a small circle of trusted coworkers. He decided to invite them for an overnight retreat at the mission guesthouse. To his pleasure three close friends accepted his invitation. Jerry was a fellow teacher in the Bible Institute. Tim was a missionary church planter, now involved in partnering with the African pastors of the district. Dan, a doctor, was the main advisor for the medical work.

The guesthouse had a comfortable meeting room that the hosts gladly made available to them. Friday afternoon the four met together. After some sharing concerning ministry, family, and news from home, John suggested they spend time in prayer for guidance. The earnestness in his voice brought seriousness to the small group. One of them mentioned later that this prayer time gave him a sense of anticipation, a conviction that the Lord had something in particular to tell them.

John spent most of the afternoon opening his heart, trying to convey concepts the Lord had impressed upon him—the missionary nature of the church, the essence of the Great Commission, the organic union of the church with her mission at Pentecost, the subsequent divorce. Relationships among those in the group were deep enough that the others listened intently. There was dialogue, an occasional "wow," periods of reflection, and statements like, "I never quite thought of things that way."

After dinner the concept of the dichotomy between the church and her mission animated the discussion. "Yes indeed, the church throughout history has known this divorce between churches and missions. And you are right, the divorce came early," remarked Jerry, whose courses at the institute included church history. "When the church became an official religion of the empire, the world became its parish rather than a mission field. The institutional church became more interested in extending its own influence than calling people from darkness to light. Fortunately the monastic orders picked up the missionary torch to some degree. Sadly, things have not changed all that much, because now the mission agencies assume the responsibility for world mission and too often the churches are there only to support them."

"I agree with John that we have two compartments in our brain, one for the church and one for mission," exclaimed Tim. Tim had spent most of his life in church planting, but was willing to admit that he had probably done as much to perpetuate the divorce in new churches as to infuse missionary vision. "Let me share an experience with you. A few years ago I was home for the Bible conference sponsored by my seminary. When I looked at the program I discovered nearly a dozen workshops on various subjects for church leaders, such as youth work, finances, counseling, and you name it. But nothing about the church's mission. Well, I went to the organizer, a friend of mine, and asked him why there was nothing concerning the church and her mission. You cannot believe his answer. He said, 'Tim, we give you missionaries a whole week during the school year for *your* conference. Why aren't you satisfied?'"

> The missionary is there mainly for financial support for his ministry, rather than encouraging the church in its mission.

"I guess that illustrates the point," exclaimed John.

Jerry broke in, "But don't you think we missionaries are as responsible as anyone for the dichotomy? Think of our missionary conferences. They are always different—so different that people cannot identify with missions like they can with other things the church does. Most other conferences try to get people involved personally in some kind of ministry. For ours, they come to admire the missionary and hear his stories, but probably realize that he is there mainly for financial support for his ministry, rather than to encourage them in their ministry."

"I suppose," said John, "that the divorce has been equally tragic both for missions *and* for the church. It has certainly had a disastrous effect on our churches. When people lose their global *vision*, they begin to lose their spiritual *vitality*. And of course all this affects their *values*. How many churches do we know where paving the parking lot becomes more important than reaching the lost?"

"Wow, you packed a lot into that one sentence," interrupted

Jerry. "But let's look at the other side of the coin," he continued. "Look at what all this has done to missions."

"Explain what you mean," said Dan.

"I'll try. If the church is the focal point of the plan of God, according to Paul in Ephesians 1, then to take the church out of missions is just as damaging as to take mission out of the church. Taking the church out of missions almost means taking missions out of the mainstream of God's great plan. If our mission agencies become mere parachurch organizations, it affects about everything we do."

There was silence. The men were trying hard to process everything that had just been said. Finally Tim spoke. "You know, it seems to me that our churches are so focused on the missionary himself that they never really become involved in the missionary's *mission*. You might say they are more concerned with what they do *for* the missionary, than what they are doing *through* the missionary."

That statement seemed to electrify John. "Say that again," he exclaimed.

"What do you mean?" replied Tim, bewildered.

"Your last sentence," continued John. "You said that churches were focused on what they were doing *for* the missionary rather than *through* the missionary."

"Well it sounds as if you don't agree," answered a confused Tim. "On the contrary," continued John, showing increased excitement. "This is precisely what we have been discussing all day. But I have never heard it put in such a concise way. You seem to have gone right to the core of the matter in a couple of words. That summarizes everything we have been saying."

Dan intervened. "But Tim is talking about the problem. He made a good diagnosis, but we are looking for the cure, aren't we?"

"Well, Doctor, you have always told me that the first step toward a cure is a proper diagnosis." This was John talking again. "Maybe in this case the cure is *in* the diagnosis. If Tim has hit on the *wrong* way for churches to look at missions, then what is the *right* way? What about turning the statement around?"

"What about saying, 'Missions is not what the church does…'"

In unison all three men cried out, *"for the missionary..."*

"That's it," said John. "Missions is not what the church does *for* the missionary but what the church does *through* the missionary."

They all realized that this simple statement, which would become their slogan, represented an entirely new way of seeing. Even though the two parts of the phrase differed only by a preposition, the new paradigm could have a revolutionary effect for those bound by the old traditions.

This would be a new way of looking at *churches*—seeing that the church, as the focal point of God's plan, is in the world to fulfill her mission, not merely to maintain her existence. This means that churches need to be proactive in the fulfillment of the Great Commission, not just reacting to appeals by missionaries.

This would be a new way of looking at *missions*—seeing that the mission of the church is to make disciples of all nations and gather them together into local communities, not merely to support missionaries. This would mean entering into a caring relationship with nations through adoption of people groups. It would also mean seeing the new mission churches as a part of their spiritual family with whom they have relationship and responsibility.

Moreover, it would be a new way of looking at the *missionary*—seeing him or her as the vital link between the church and the nations of the world and an indispensable element for fulfilling the church's mission through teamwork. The missionary would not merely be someone who comes occasionally to share about *his* work in order to gain financial support. Churches would learn to see mission agencies as partners in the Great Commission, serving local churches by allowing them to do together what they would not be able to do alone.

⌒Chapter Five⌒

PLANNING FOR ACTION

The previous evening's excitement was still evident when the four men gathered around the breakfast table. The concept of missions as what the church could do *through* the missionary was stirring their thinking. New insights began to sprout as they related this concept to their experience with their churches. The coming hours promised to be full and intense.

After a particularly rich time of prayer, John again took the lead.

"When we say that missions is what the church does *through*, rather than *for* the missionary, we speak out of a background of experience that makes those words more than a slogan. I think we all understand that this will not be the case when we try to explain these concepts to the people in the churches who support us."

"In fact, the slogan may not even have much meaning for a few of the people sitting back in the offices of our mission agencies," added Tim. "How can we help this make sense to the people back home?"

"Above all, let's keep it simple," exclaimed Dan, the doctor. "When I treat people, my interest is their healing rather than teaching them medical science. Of course I try to explain why certain medicines will work and what they do, but my main challenge is to get them to *take* the medicine. If they take it they will have the results, whether they understand or not."

"Well Doctor Dan, what kind of pills do you prescribe for *churches* that are sick?" John was only half joking when he asked that question, realizing it sounded a bit cynical.

Dan was not discouraged. "Before prescribing the pills you need more than a good diagnosis of the problem; people have to be *convinced* that they need treatment. It is the same for our churches. They will have to be convinced they have needs in order for them to look for solutions."

"It is evident that they do not need more programs." It was Jerry's turn. "Some of the pastors I know are sick of trying to make new programs work. Programs seem to stifle whatever life is left, because it is always the few dedicated people, already over-worked, that get stuck with them. Sometimes I think we forget that a church is supposed to be an organism, where programs grow out of relationships, rather than primarily an organization, where we try to cause relationships to grow out of programs. We cannot squeeze churches into molds. Change is going to have to be from inside out, rather than outside in."

"All this sounds good," said Tim, "but how do you do it? On the one hand we are saying that people are going to have to become involved—they must do something. Then we are saying that we do not want to involve them in new programs. It looks as if we are on a dead end street."

"Maybe we are making this too hard." John felt it was time to move ahead. "Let's try to do what Dan mentioned: make a diagnosis to see what the needs are. Maybe we can look at those needs through our new slogan, 'Missions is not what the church does *for,* but *through* the missionary.' Maybe this will help us look at things from the inside out rather than the outside in."

Jerry picked up the suggestion. "If we are talking about *needs,* there is no question in my mind about where we should start. Our churches need new *vision,* vision that will give them a sense of ownership. I think you should measure the potential of a church by its vision, not by how many are sitting in the pews on Sunday morning. In other words, its *sending* capacity rather than its *seating* capacity. When I get into some churches I almost have the impression I am in a house without windows, as if everything is focused inward on the people and their concerns and that there is no world out there.

"I must say that when I began my ministry I didn't do much to help the situation, because I guess I was only interested in my own little world. If they kept writing out the checks I was satisfied. At some point I realized the Lord was sending me into those churches for a greater purpose—I had a mission to the churches as well as to people here in Africa. I began to see that *I* had to be their window, to open their eyes to a part of the world they had not seen before."

The nods around the table indicated agreement with Jerry's impassioned words.

John continued, "Right, but how does vision work itself out in change? If we say that missions is what the church *does* through the missionary, the people cannot just sit around looking at each other. They have to *do* something. This certainly means more than merely reacting to appeals, because this would be doing it *for* and not *through* the missionary. Rather than *react to appeals*, churches will have to learn how to *respond to needs*. For this to happen, the churches will have to be able to bring some focus to their vision."

"It sounds as if you are talking about setting goals," said Jerry. "Are we getting back into the program mold? I know some people who think that goal setting is pretty legalistic, and in fact that goal setting can quench the Spirit. They think that if you don't make the goal, it is a pretty good indication you were out of God's will when you set it."

"Come off it, Jerry. It's not the *goals* that are legalistic; it is that too many *people* become legalistic in the way they try to keep them. Goals are what you aim for, not necessarily what you hit. Everyone sets goals all the time. I'll bet even *you* become goal-oriented when you buy an airline ticket." Tim was beginning to enjoy the freedom the four men were feeling in their relationship, and even Jerry had to laugh at his last remark. John again picked up the conversation.

"I think we would all admit that goals are basic to teamwork. They bring motivation because they give us a way of measuring progress and results. I cannot imagine a soccer game being played without goals. Maybe the lack of real goals in missions is one of the main reasons many Christians do not feel much excitement.

"The main thing about having a plan with goals is that it tells us where to go, like a map. The more I meditate on Acts 1:8, which is like a prism breaking down the peoples of the world into four distinct parts, the more I realize that some kind of map is necessary if the church is to fulfill her God-given commission to be a witness in the entire world."

> A map is... a picture of reality that allows us to make intelligent decisions... and to measure our progress. A map... frees us for action.

"I hear what you are saying," interrupted Dan, "but I also heard something else that maybe you did not say. You said a plan with goals is like a map. When you said that, a light went on in my mind. Any map is supposed to answer three questions: where I am, where I am going, and how do I get there? Aren't these the three questions every church needs to answer if it is going to become proactive in its mission?

"A map is not a program imposed upon us; it is a picture of reality that allows us to make intelligent decisions on the basis of our destination, and to measure our progress. A map does not squeeze us into a mold; it frees us for action."

"An action plan," interjected Tim.

"A Mission Action Plan," added Jerry.

"Well what about that! You have even come up with an acronym. And for once it's an acronym that fits. Every church needs a MAP, to help them find out where they are, to help them focus on a destination, and to guide them in determining what is the best way to get there. Bravo!" John shouted. And he wasted no time in continuing.

"Now we are talking about something that is *really* an inside-out approach. If we want churches to become proactive—to respond to needs rather than appeals—they will have to start where they are. Present commitments become the springboard for future involvement. Most churches know the names of the missionaries they support, but not very many are acquainted with the ministries they are involved in. Churches have trophy cases for winning the volleyball tournament, but have no idea of what kind of church-planting victories their team has had. You always have to start where you are.

"But in a deeper way, if churches are going to fulfill their mission, they will have to begin to discover their potential. Every church is unique, and has a unique potential for global mission. I remember stopping by a new church to visit with the young man who had pioneered the effort. As we talked he said, 'Well, things are going pretty well. We have worked hard trying to reach our Jerusalem. Now I guess we need to start thinking about supporting a missionary.'

"You know what I said? I just said, 'I guess so.'

"I wish I had another try at that conversation. I should have said, 'Why would you do that?' I should have told him that the first step is to discover the *mission* of the church, and then maybe the next step would be to support a *missionary*. And to discover your mission you will have to look at your potential.'"

"John, you are making sense," said Jerry. "I am sorry to say that I never exactly saw it in that way. I guess you could call this the *research* phase of planning. And of course that is only the starting point. Good research will probably result in focused vision—the *vision* phase of planning—when churches begin to realize that their mission is not to support missionaries, but to make disciples."

"Which leads us to the *action* phase." It was Dan's turn. "And maybe if we have made progress on the research and vision phases, we will not have to formulate a complicated plan answering in detail all the *why, what, how, when,* and *who* questions before we start moving. All we have to answer, at any point of time, is *what is the next step?* When I pull out my map and start out, I make decisions one at a time on the basis of where I am going. If I had to think through every curve and turn I probably would not even start."

"We need a break, guys," said John. "But first let me tell you how encouraging this has been to me. What you are describing this morning is far different from the complicated policy manuals that so many churches seem to be fascinated with now. You are describing a workable, simple plan. Policies tell us what we can and can't do, but plans tell us where we are going."

"Let's pick this up in a half hour."

ᗒ Chapter Six ᗕ

TEAMWORK

John took a brief walk during the break. Few discussions had been as helpful for him as the one he had just experienced. He knew that they were on the right track—for churches to become proactive, to get out of the maintenance mode and into the mission mode, they must have a destination. He remembered a trip made some years ago to California, seeing the majestic Queen Mary in the Long Beach harbor, so beautiful and yet so sad. Here was an ocean liner built to sail the open seas now being used as a reception hall. To be sure, sailing the ocean required far more maintenance than hosting parties, but it was maintenance with a purpose.

To get out of the maintenance mode churches would have to learn to think strategically—to relate their activities to vision and goals. But would they—or could they? Planning is hard work. Putting a plan together is far more difficult than formulating a policy. Plans force you to launch out into the unexplored; they require commitment; there is a risk factor. Tracing boundaries is always easier than making goals.

He realized also that without prayers for God's guidance, plans can be worthless. He thought of Proverbs 16:9: "In his heart a man plans his course, but the Lord determines his steps." Or Proverbs 19:21: "Many are the plans in a man's heart, but it is the Lord's purpose that prevails." Plans must grow out of prayer. But they must also lead to prayer. At this point an entirely new idea came to him. *Maybe one of the main purposes of focused planning is focused prayer!*

Further, plans are useless unless committed people work hard to implement them. *"Plans don't work. It is the people who work. Plans bring people together in teamwork."*

This thought primed him for the continuing discussion. The other three were already around the table. "Suppose the churches are able to do some good planning and come up with a workable MAP—a Mission Action Plan. What is necessary to make the plan work—to implement it?" he asked.

> Plans don't work. It is the people who work. Plans bring people together in teamwork.

Three voices responded in unison: "People." John realized that his thinking was not so original after all.

"Okay," he continued, deciding not to show surprise at the unison of their response. "How do you get the people involved?"

"Well," said Tim, "I suppose most people would say you should elect a committee. At least that seems to be what most churches do. I remember that some years ago there was an effort to encourage our churches to put together a missions committee. Now some of the churches I am in contact with are wondering how to work *around* their missions committee. Some of these committees have done little more than intensify the divorce between the church and her mission. They've marginalized the Great Commission, too often putting it in the hands of people who are not on the inside track in the church body."

Dan spoke. "When you talk about committees, it seems that most people really have to be pushed before they are willing to serve. Then when they accept, they usually have no particular duties except to attend the meetings. They generally come to the meetings without much background about what they are going to discuss. They leave without being given any responsibilities. If they want to feel some sense of identity, the only way they can function is to say something during the meeting. Usually their remarks are more focused on problems rather than potential. Some of the committees I have served on have certainly shown talent in stifling vision."

John picked up the thought. "You know, some of the same people who seem negative on a committee might come alive if they were placed in a different context. *What if they knew they were chosen because of their skills and commitment, rather than because no one else was willing to serve?* What if they were joined to the others because of some common goals that everyone was excited about? What if each had a role to play that they knew was essential to the success of the group? What if they had a leader who saw them not as obstacles to his personal plans, but players who were indispensable for the fulfillment of the vision?"

"Hey," piped up Dan. "You are not talking about a committee. You are describing a team."

"Precisely," responded John. "A team. A team with common goals, defined roles, and visionary leadership. To implement a Mission Action Plan, churches are going to need a Mission Action Team. A team committed to mission and focused on action."

"So we have discovered another acronym," said Tim with a sly glance at the others, who knew immediately what he was referring to. "A MAP is one thing; a MAT is something else. In Africa a mat doesn't exactly imply action."

"Forget it," John pursued. "Call it what you will. We all know that a team is as different from a committee as day from night. You know, in practically every church we have people who are highly skilled but who are untapped resources with respect to the Great Commission. We just do not get them mobilized for missions because the great divorce has trapped us in our traditions, where missions belong to the professional missionary. We see missions only as something the church does *for* the missionary, and that usually is limited to the support commitment and a few promises for prayer that may or may not be serious. All this time the church has people, sometimes highly successful in their fields, who would love nothing more than to know that they could invest their competence in eternal matters with global impact.

"We get the concept," said the others. "Let's spell it out a little more."

"Okay," said John. "Let's do it together. Suppose a church has put together a good Mission Action Plan, really seeking to unleash the resources of the church for their simultaneous witness in their Jerusalem, Judea, Samaria, and the ends of the earth. What are some of the needs that must be met in order to see this implemented?"

"I suppose we ought to start with the obvious." This was Jerry. "You would need a leader. You would need someone who knows where he is going and can motivate others to go with him. He would have to be good with both plans and people, in addition to being really committed to the Lord and the Great Commission."

"How would you go about finding that person in the church?" pursued John.

"Well, I guess you would need to look for someone who already has some experience in leading."

"Precisely. This is the whole idea. If we have a particular need, let's look for the people who are already gifted, trained, and skilled to meet that need. Let's see if they sense the leading of the Lord to offer themselves and their talents for something that is right at the core of what God is doing in the world, something that means building with gold, silver, and precious stones, rather than wood, hay, and stubble."

"I get it." Now it was Tim's turn. "A good leader will look for the best people available to do the jobs that need to be done. That means if we want to *educate* the church in the Mission Action Plan, we need to look for the best *educator* in the church. Educators are in our churches in abundance, but most of them do not relate their profession to global missions. Just think of what would happen if the church would challenge one of its gifted educators to formulate a plan for educating the entire congregation in the Mission Action Plan—children, youth, and adults—with whatever methods are the most effective, and with a budget that would make this possible!"

Everyone began to jump into the conversation. "How about *finances?* Frankly, some of the mission financial policies of my supporting churches are pathetic. The best minds of the church do not seem to get into the mission side of the finances. Some of our churches have financial planners who probably would be able to double the missions giving of the church just by doing some estate planning with a few of the families, to say nothing of teaching them the principles of faith giving. You know, if some of these men would team up with some of the newer missionaries in helping them raise support, it might give the missionaries an entirely different perspective of the churches. It would certainly send them to the field with a more positive attitude."

As each area of need was identified, the four men agreed that most of their supporting churches included people who would be competent to meet those needs. If properly mobilized, they would be a big factor in bringing life to the churches. They also agreed that the divorce between the church and her mission had put blinders on the eyes of the church's leadership with respect to the potential of these people.

At a certain point in the conversation Dan spoke up. "The more we talk about a Mission Action Team, the more I see it somewhat as a pyramid, divided into six blocks. At the top, the point of the pyramid, is the leader, or the coordinator. If we really believe that mission is the essential purpose of the church, I suppose that in some churches the coordinator would have to be the pastor. If not, it would certainly be the pastor's right hand man. He would be the person who combines vision, organizational skills, and good relationships.

"The foundation of the pyramid would be divided into three parts that would correspond with our age-old slogan in missions: 'pray, give, and go.' We would need a superb prayer coordinator, someone who would snoop around in all the groups and activities of the church to see if global intercession has been integrated. That person would also see that prayer groups are both organized and functioning.

"We have already talked about the giving coordinator. But we also need a coordinator for *mobilizing* people for mission. This would be someone who can see the mission as the DNA of the

church, can see the world through the Acts 1:8 paradigm, and can
see the potential in everyone.

"Then in the middle, you would have two people holding the
pyramid together. One would be the mission education coordinator. The other, a program coordinator, would keep the calendar,
schedule and organize events, and coordinate the visits of missionaries. What a difference it would make if before we visit a church
someone would be giving thought and prayer about how our visit
could be maximized!"

All three men knew that Dan had identified the six essential
functions to implement a Mission Action Plan. Whether the
people filling those responsibilities were called a team, a task force,
a commission—or even a committee—they would have to be dedicated people willing to use their gifts for the Lord. They would
have to be led by someone with vision.

The pyramid idea "clicked."

Chapter Seven

TOTAL MOBILIZATION

Even though the sun was at its hottest, all four men decided to take a brief walk after lunch. John knew of a spot near the missionary guesthouse where trees lined the road.

Talk was sparse. The morning's discussion had been pretty intense, and the men were trying to digest the ideas that had come out of their exchanges. It was hard work.

Dan broke the silence. "You know, I've been thinking about the church being the body of Christ. I guess you realize I know a little bit about the human body. Since the Lord used the body as a metaphor of His church, there are bound to be a lot of comparisons between the two.

"I was just thinking of what is happening to our own bodies while we are out here walking. We can live for several weeks without food, but without oxygen we will die in a matter of minutes. That's true of cells as well as the body as a whole. A healthy body needs exercise. The physical effort we are expending right now is pushing more blood into the capillaries, which means that our cells are being nourished with oxygen.

"When we don't exercise, our bodies become lethargic. Do you suppose that there is a comparison between aerobics and the church's involvement in the Great Commission?"

"Great analogy," John replied. "People in the church are a little like the cells of the body. When the Spirit of mission is quenched, they become dysfunctional. Getting the church active in mission is like spiritual aerobics, forcing life into all its parts."

Jerry picked up the thought. "What you have just said tells me that *every* member of the church needs to be mobilized for its mission—not just the missionaries the church sends to other countries. If the Great Commission is for all believers, then everyone ought to be involved in one way or another."

"Total mobilization," they thought as they headed back.

> Reuniting the church with her mission means challenging *every member* to become involved... with the church's global outreach.

At the mission house their prayer time was even more intense. Total mobilization. What does that mean? Were they dreaming, or is it possible to think that every member, in one way or another, could find a place in the Acts 1:8 mission of the church? Saying that missions is what the church does *through* the missionary means that the church as a whole is supposed to be involved. Dan was right. Unless the church as a complete body is functioning according to the desires of the head, stagnation is bound to creep in.

Total mobilization. Just what would that mean in the average church?

"I think we all understand that total mobilization certainly does not mean that everyone would be doing the same thing," said Jerry. "Somehow people get the idea that unless you are sent by a mission agency to another country you are not involved in missions. We certainly don't have that idea when we think about countries engaged in war. The number of soldiers actually sent to the front lines is small in comparison to the total number of people involved one way or another in the conflict.

"People involved in a war do all kinds of things. But they all realize what they are doing has meaning because it is a part of the war effort, and if they don't do a good job, their failure will affect the war effort in some way. It's not too hard to realize that those who are praying and giving are contributing directly to the spiritual war effort. Maybe we need to realize that any ministry in the church can be a part of the war effort."

"With one big condition," interjected Tim. "That's only true when the church is turned outward in mission, and the people know what the mission is. When a country goes to war, all the citizens know it. The media is full of it every day. People are willing to make all kinds of sacrifices if they know they are contributing to the war effort."

It was Jerry's turn. "But you know, none of those things would have any meaning if no one was on the front lines personally engaged with the enemy. I think we would all agree that we can be involved in missions in whatever we do. But without missionaries total mobilization would be meaningless.

"Let's come back to the missionary. It seems to me that the main focus of missions still has to be the missionary. If a church doesn't have any missionaries, how can we say that it is on mission?

"But do we agree on *who* is a missionary," said John. "Some people would say that *every* Christian is a missionary, and in one way that's true, because we are all *sent ones*. But that pretty much makes the term meaningless. On the other hand, we all agree that we can't limit that term just to the professionals, the missionaries sent by a mission agency to somewhere else in the world.

"Let me make a stab at another definition of missionary, in light of what we have just said concerning total mobilization. Let's say that a missionary is not necessarily someone who goes from one country to another. *A missionary is someone who is sent from the church to the world.*"

"Explain that."

"A missionary is someone commissioned by the church to fulfill a disciple-making mission outside the scope of the existing church. This means that a missionary can be *anyone* in the church, regardless of his position or level of training. It means that a missionary can be someone sent to *any of the four people groups* of Acts 1:8. It also means that a missionary can be commissioned for *any period of time.*

"I think that we have learned from Acts 13:1-3 that it is the church that provides the context for mobilizing missionaries. When the entire church is educated in the Mission Action Plan, the people of the church will begin to realize that if the church is on *mission* in the world, then many of them will have to commit themselves as *missionaries*.

"This does not mean of course that they will all dedicate the remainder of their lives for service in another country. It means that for whatever mission the church undertakes in its Jerusalem, Judea, Samaria, or to the ends of the earth, missionaries will be required. Some will be commissioned to create a spiritual community in a mobile home court. Some, who are in business, will be commissioned to use their business trip abroad to fulfill a particular mission of the church. Some will be sent on short-term teams.

> A *missionary* is *anyone*, no matter what his age or status in the church, who is commissioned for *any defined mission* that grows out of the mission of the church.

"Anyone sent out by the church, whether to another part of town or to the other side of the globe, whether sent for two weeks or two years, whether supported by the church or self-supported, is a missionary, and needs to be commissioned by the church. Those of us who are career missionaries have been commissioned, and we know that commissioning has profound meaning. It is not only a sign of the anointing of the Spirit for a particular calling, but also of the commitment of the church to that ministry. It is unfortunate that laying on of hands has usually been limited to those we call career missionaries."

"John, you have said a mouthful." Three heads nodded at Tim's response. "If I understand what you are saying, what you have done is bring the local church into the center of things—*to define the term missionary in relation to the local church.* I like that. It goes along perfectly with everything we have been saying, starting with

Acts 13. In other words, a *missionary* is *anyone,* no matter what his age or status in the church, who is commissioned for *any defined mission* that grows out of the mission of the church, and sent *anywhere,* whether it is in the church's Jerusalem, Judea, Samaria, or the ends of the earth."

"By the way," commented Dan as they were leaving for a cup of coffee. "In view of what the church is, and in view of what the world is, can you think of any mission of the church to the world which is *not* cross cultural to one degree or another?"

Chapter Eight

GETTING IN S.T.E.P.

Only a couple of hours remained until the men would have to return home. All had responsibilities on Sunday. John was anxious to tie things together—to try to pull together some of the points that had come up in their discussion and to put them in order.

That's why he initially did not react with too much enthusiasm when Tim said, "There is something we have not discussed yet."

"You mean after all we have talked about there are still things we have to discuss?" thought John, not wanting to say it out loud. And he was glad he kept quiet when Tim spoke one word.

"Prayer."

"For all our good ideas about Mission Action Plans, Mission Action Teams and even World Mission Churches, nothing is going to happen in the long run without prayer. I once heard someone say that without prayer we can benefit from the *providence* of God, but if we want to know His *intervention,* we have to pray."

John felt a twinge of guilt. He knew from his own experience with God that nothing was more fascinating than prayer. He knew that at any time, any place, or under any circumstances, he could talk personally with the One who had sent him to Africa and had created the universe. He could come to God under any circumstances and have His complete attention.

Tim continued the conversation. "I used to wonder why we have so many commands to pray when God knows all along what is needed. Then I realized that He still wants to get the credit for what He does. Sometimes at the end of the day I feel like a little god myself, pulling all the strings and trying to make everything happen. Then I realize I am ruling over a pitifully small kingdom, and I had better move things back into His hands."

"You know something," said Dan. "My computer has taught me a few things about prayer. Before the information highway was ever thought of, the intercession highway was in full swing. The software is right between our ears, the password is Jesus, we can access anywhere in the world, and we have unlimited time."

Of course that brought a laugh, but the truth of the analogy made an impact. As they continued to talk, they all expressed agreement that if there is anything indispensable to missions it is prayer. They agreed that many churches—as well as some missionaries—give lip service to discussing prayer, rather than praying. Encouraging focused prayer was their main challenge; what could be done to make prayer ministries more effective?

> If there is anything indispensable to missions, it is prayer.

Jerry asked for their attention. "I just remembered a little experience I had several years ago that might have some bearing on what we are discussing. I was at a retreat where some pastors had invited several missionaries to discuss some of the same things we are talking about. During the afternoon we divided into small groups. One of the pastors in our group asked the missionaries what had been the most helpful thing churches had done for their ministries.

"We all thought for awhile and then one of the missionaries began to share about a relationship he had made with a man in one of his supporting churches. This man had offered himself to be the homeland partner of the missionary, and the missionary sensed that the offer was more than a desire to please. During the years that followed a deep relationship developed between the two. Whenever the missionary needed help, whether advice or something more tangible, his partner was there. After several years the partner visited the missionary where he was serving and the relationship became even deeper.

"I was just thinking. What if a missionary had someone like that in each of his supporting churches—an individual or a couple? But someone focused on prayer. Sometimes I get discouraged that my churches don't write to me; then I remind myself that churches don't use computers—people do. If a church is a family rather than an institution, then I have to develop personal relationships within the family. I have been so used to thinking of committees and budgets when I think of my churches, that sometimes I forget the people. I think I would like to start developing a personal relationship with one person, or couple, in each of my churches—as a communication link, mainly for prayer."

"If the idea is good, why not have several partners?" asked Tim.

John interrupted. "Just a minute. The Chinese say that if more than one person feeds the same mule, the mule will die of hunger. And we all know that if more than one missionary services the same car, the engine will soon burn out. So, there must be one responsible prayer partner who may enlist others to pray, of course."

"Well said." Tim needed to talk. "I think that we are onto a great idea. I can hardly imagine engineers building a power plant for houses equipped with electrical appliances, then forgetting to put a power line to the houses. Not only would the partner be in communication with the missionary, he would also be in communication with the church. He would be the one to organize a prayer group for the missionary and his ministry within the church. The partner would be our Epaphroditus, like in Philippians 2:25."

"Let me add another idea to this," said Dan, excitedly. "It seems to me that if the partner is given a particular mission to fulfill, just as the missionary is, then the partner needs to be commissioned in some way just like the missionary. In fact, some of us have never been commissioned in our supporting churches; that was done by the mission agency. Maybe we could encourage the churches to commission us and our partners together."

Dusk comes early near the equator. The men did not need watches to know that their time was coming to a close.

"This has been a rich time together," stated John. "I really appreciate your being willing to consecrate this time for what I am seeing is going to be my main passion in the ministry, trying to bring back together what God never meant to be separated, the church and her mission. Our discussions have given me a lot to chew on, and it might take a long time to digest it. I wish we could have tied things together before we left, but I guess each of us will have to do that on his own. It might take some time to build this into some kind of structure, but we sure have a lot of material to put into it: Mission Action Plans, Mission Action Teams, World Mission Churches, and now Partners in Prayer."

"Wait. I've got an idea!" Dan's outburst almost stunned the others. "We've had some fun with acronyms, but maybe we have come up with the best one yet. Do you realize what we have done? We have come up with a process for getting our churches in S.T.E.P. with the Great Commission."

The other three looked bewildered. They sat in silence.

"Listen to me," continued an excited Dan. "A Mission Action Plan—that's a strategy, isn't it? A strategy does not have to be something complicated. It is simply a plan defining some goals and tracing out ways to reach them. And with what letter does 'Strategy' begin? Precisely, an 'S.'

"We all agreed that strategies don't work themselves; it is the people who work the strategies. Committees don't cut it, because people on committees do not have a sense of personal responsibility for the goals. What you need is a team, a loyal group of people with common goals, defined roles, and visionary leadership. And gentlemen, 'Team' begins with the letter 'T.'

"That brings us to mobilization, realizing that if the Great Commission is given to the church as a whole, then the whole church needs to be mobilized for its mission. The mission is not 'over there,' it is right here. If a church does its planning well, looking at its resources as a first step, before formulating its objectives, then it will have to mobilize its people. To mobilize is to enlist. Do you get it? Enlistment. The letter 'E.'

"And if Tim had not laid the foundation for everything else we have discussed, we may have gone away simply assuming that since we all believe that prayer is indispensable, it would just happen automatically without having to be structured into the MAP. Without the letter 'P' we would have been left hanging. But now you know what I meant when I said we can get our churches in S.T.E.P. with the Great Commission."

"Ingenious," spoke Jerry, somewhat tongue in cheek. "I'm glad we didn't end with 'work' instead of 'prayer.' Then we would have all been in a stew."

"Awful." John knew it was time for their discussion to end. Everything was starting to be funny. But he also knew that Dan had stumbled onto something that might prove very helpful as a communication tool for these concepts. Whether or not the churches would go for the S.T.E.P. process as a tool for bringing back together what God had never intended should be separated, John knew that it would be a tool for him.

John brought things to a close. "Gentlemen, it is time to pray. I want you to know that this overnight retreat has been more helpful than I can tell you. I really appreciate your willingness to spend this time. I personally believe that we are going to see some significant changes in our churches—and in us—as a result."

Strategy
Teamwork
Enlistment
Prayer

Chapter Nine

OPENING THE PASTOR'S EYES

Now we return to John's first Sunday back at Hillside and pick up the story where we left it. Having learned what happened to John during the weeks preceding his return, we now have an understanding of the bluntness of his memorable message to the people of Hillside Community Church.

John had not slept well the Sunday night after his message. His mind kept racing through what he had said. At breakfast, after a cup of coffee, he nursed some second thoughts about the wisdom of being so direct—and for bringing so much confusion to the people.

He felt the slap of reality on his face. Bouncing ideas back and forth with his missionary friends had been fun. Facing people who would have to implement them was moving him onto a new and unfamiliar playing field. As he reviewed his message, he knew that he had probably gone too far and had hit them broadside. He had not taken the time to prepare the people—or the pastor. This made him a bit apprehensive about what would happen when he saw Pastor Smith. He wondered what his pastor was thinking. They hadn't yet made contact.

He did not have to speculate very long. The phone rang. It was Pastor Smith. Though he usually took Monday off, he could not get John's remarks off his mind. He was not comfortable with his thoughts.

"Your message surprised me, John, and some of the things you said have bothered me. I began wondering whether you were calling my ministry into question, and I can see now why you almost insisted on seeing me before you spoke.

"But the more I think about your message, the more I realize that maybe you said some things I should listen to. In fact I wonder if some of the struggles we are having here may be related to issues deeper than I had realized. I would really like to get together with you and pursue these things. Could you meet me for lunch?"

At the restaurant Pastor Smith did not wait until lunch was served to begin his questioning. "You referred to a number of Scripture passages yesterday morning, John. You know, I have preached on some of those passages for years, but I guess I saw them simply as things that happened in the past rather than truths related to my church and me. Of course I know that the Great Commission is for all Christians, but after all, we have been supporting you for a number of years now and so I felt pretty good about that one."

"Don't think that you are any different from most pastors," John replied. "Or missionaries. I have been a missionary for many years but only in the last few weeks have I have begun to see things the way I shared them yesterday. We have become so accustomed to the divorce between the church and her mission that most of us are no longer uncomfortable about it. In fact, I have to confess that we missionaries have probably done as much to perpetuate the divorce as anyone. We seem to delight in making our ministries so different that few people can relate personally to them." John found himself repeating some of the statements made by his three friends.

When the waitress brought the sandwiches, Pastor Smith was polite enough to allow John to finish eating before the heavy conversation started, but it was evident that he wanted to get right to the point. "I had the impression during your message that you were just giving us the tip of the iceberg, and there is a lot more to be said. Tell me more about this divorce."

John paused to collect his thoughts, finish his last french fry, and settle back in his chair to begin what turned out to be a lengthy discourse. He realized that discussing these thoughts with his three friends had been easier than trying to relate them to his own pastor. In Africa it was almost fun to put ideas into neat little patterns.

Now he would have to face the reality of a typical church that for years had suffered the consequences of basically being turned inward. He also knew that if he could not help his own pastor apply these concepts to his own church, there was not much chance they would succeed elsewhere.

He decided to begin by trying to paint the big picture. He talked in detail about the two encounters of Jesus with His disciples, two streams that came together on the day of Pentecost to form a mighty river.

"Okay," interrupted Pastor Smith, "but what about the divorce?"

"Well," said John, remembering Jerry's explanation back in Africa, "it occurred a long time ago when churches lost sight of their heavenly citizenship and became preoccupied with extending their earthly influence. For us today, the situation is different. Probably the main consequence of the divorce is that the mission of the church is usually relegated to specialized agencies. Mission involvement is measured by financial commitment.

"Don't get me wrong. I am certainly not criticizing mission agencies. I thank God for the one I serve with. Not many churches can do it on their own. Thank God for anyone, during any period of history, who has picked up the torch for evangelism and missions and in the name of the Lord Jesus has gone into areas were the gospel has not been heard.

"Nevertheless, no one can escape the effects of divorce. The divorce between churches and their mission has had consequences far more profound than most of us realize—both on missionaries and on the churches who support us.

"As I said yesterday morning, and I'm sorry for being so blunt, many missionaries are a little like spiritual orphans with respect to local churches. You have shown a lot of interest in me, but you know as well as I that my real relationships are with my mission agency rather than the church. If you were to ask many missionaries who their pastor is, someone who really cares about them and gives them spiritual help, they would have to shake their heads sadly and say they have none. They find it difficult to identify one church among many to which they feel any spiritual accountability. They can talk easily about their *supporting* churches. But it is often a different question when they seek to identify their *sending,* or *sustaining* church.

"This not only manifests itself in spiritual loneliness; it can in fact often result in a spiritual independence that is detrimental to the ministry, and in some cases even spiritually dangerous. Many missionaries go into battle with their heads uncovered. It seems evident that the spiritual power necessary for the fulfillment of our ministry is supposed to come through the church, according to Ephesians 1:22-23. Of course, the mission agency tries to assume the role of the church in the life of the missionary. But is this God's plan? Is it an adequate substitute?"

Pastor Smith interrupted. "But John, what you are describing is something that I doubt our church is capable of doing. Further, I personally do not see myself as capable of fulfilling the role of pastor to someone like you. After all, *you* are the missionary. I'm just a simple pastor. We aren't the experts; your mission agency is *supposed* to be caring for you."

"Pastor Smith," said John gravely, "sure, the mission agency has a role to play, and it is doing it well, but what I am trying to say is that no agency can replace the church. If missions is what the church does *through* the missionary and not just *for* the missionary, that means that the mission agency must assume more of a servant role toward the church, and the church must take more initiative, rather than just remaining passive. As I tried to explain yesterday morning, missions must grow out of the church, rather than being grafted on. When the church shifts to an agency its spiritual responsibility for the missionary, both the church and the missionary are losers.

"Let me say something that might be hard for you to hear. When a body ceases to do what it is supposed to do, it gradually becomes dysfunctional. You see, both the missionary *and* the church are suffering the consequences of the divorce. Don't think that I have come to stand in judgment on my own church. That's not my role. But Pastor, to the extent that churches turn inward they become spiritually dysfunctional to one degree or another. When they leave the mission mode and slip into maintenance, they are bound to suffer spiritual apathy."

Pastor Smith was silent for several minutes.

"Maybe what you are saying strikes closer to home than you realize. You may as well know that things could be going better here. We have a wonderful group of people, and I think that they accept me as their pastor. But I spend most of my time just meeting people's needs. When I resolve one problem two more are on the waiting list. The older folks talk about the sense of purpose that they felt when the church began, but they don't seem to have it now. I have to admit it would be hard for me this morning to think of any purpose in my ministry other than just holding things together and keeping them going. Now you are talking about our church doing something that, frankly, I think we are incapable of doing. You are even implying that our church is dysfunctional, and that hurts. But if what you say is true, how on earth did we get this way?"

John realized they had reached a critical point in their conversation. He tried to put himself in Pastor Smith's shoes, and feel what the pastor was feeling. He spoke softly, and his voice became more gentle.

Until now the pastor had been concerned about getting the people of the world into the church [rather than] getting the people of the church into the world.

"Maybe a little story will help. Do you remember when the church gave you and your wife a trip to Israel? I am sure you visited Israel's two bodies of water—the Sea of Galilee and the Dead Sea. You probably also went up to Caesarea Philippi and saw the springs that produce the Jordan River, the river that feeds those two seas.

"Though the water comes from the same source, it would be hard to imagine two bodies of water more different. The Sea of Galilee is filled with fish. The Dead Sea is exactly what its name says—dead. Over a period of centuries the mineral impurities have accumulated to a degree that no life can be sustained.

"The difference in the two bodies of water is not the result of what flows into them, but in what flows out. The Dead Sea died because there was no outlet. Rather than flowing into the parched land of the south, watering the land and producing gardens that would bring sustenance to the population, the water simply evaporated and disappeared into the air.

"Tragically, this is the spiritual state of many churches. The fresh water of the Word has flowed into them, but in too many cases commitment to their mission has been lacking. There is no outlet and the Spirit of Christ is quenched. His Spirit is the Spirit of life; only in the fullness of His Spirit can life be sustained."

Pastor Smith sat silent.

Until now he had been concerned about getting the people of the world into the church, but had shown little or no concern about getting the people of the church into the world.

His church had gradually become a basin, rather than a base, a collection agency rather than a sending agency. He had seen the people as plants to be watered rather than seeds to be planted.

Chapter Ten

CHURCH AND AGENCY

Pastor Smith had promised to pick up his wife no later than 2:30 PM, which meant that their luncheon meeting ended abruptly. "John, I *must* see you tomorrow," he said as he was paying the cashier. "Can you come to the church?"

Shortly after nine o'clock the following day John dropped in at Pastor Smith's office. John sensed that the slight agitation in the pastor's opening remarks was not prompted by disagreement, but by confusion.

"John," began Pastor Smith, "the things you told me yesterday have been pretty sobering, but in spite of my discouragement I can see a tiny glimmer of hope. The idea that the root of our problems might be related to the divorce between our church and her mission does make sense. If somehow we can start helping people focus on the world instead of themselves, maybe we will be able to rediscover a sense of purpose that we have not had for years.

"You must realize, though, that you are pushing me out into uncharted waters. On the one hand I have the impression that nothing you are saying is all that new. But when I start to think about these things, it seems that *everything* you are saying is new. I am confused. Are you saying that we need to turn our church into a mission agency?"

"Pastor," said John, "maybe we are getting ahead of ourselves. It is true that I have been giving you the tip of the iceberg, as you said yesterday. Let's go a little deeper and try to put some things in context.

"No, I am certainly not suggesting that our church become a missionary agency. The church has one role to play and the mission agency another. What I have been trying to say is that churches have shifted just about everything concerning missions into the hands of mission agencies. After the church writes out its monthly check to the agency, it doesn't have much else to do. Not very many churches realize that they can, under God, develop plans in global mission that will allow them to recapture some initiative. Then they will see the agency as something God has raised up to partner with them in implementing their common vision.

"You see, one of the consequences of this divorce between the church and her mission is the failure to develop any kind of *real* teamwork between local churches and mission agencies. When churches become content to shift all their responsibilities onto the mission agencies, the agencies easily become autonomous, trying to play the role both of the church and an administrative institution. As we saw yesterday, the church increasingly loses vitality.

"I guess we both realize that for the most part churches such as ours have been content to let the agency take over. In fact, *most* churches are like ours—they depend on mission agencies. Of course, sometimes larger churches get the idea they can do everything on their own and no longer need to team up with the agencies. They jump from dependence to complete *independence,* acting like their own mission board. When churches try to do everything on their own, it usually creates confusion. Teamwork can occur only when the church and the agency both understand their roles, so there can be a spirit of *interdependence*—understanding that they need each other.

"Pastor, that is one of the big areas that has occupied my thinking during the past few weeks. I keep asking myself just how I need to relate to my church on the one hand, and to my mission agency on the other.

"I think I have had an excellent relationship with both. But on the other hand, the church of Antioch in Acts 13 is supposed to be our *model,* as I understand it. Perhaps we should revisit the Antioch story. In the Acts passage the church takes the initiative. I can see that I have been content to allow my church to play a passive role. I have been content to allow the mission agency to become my church. We need to rekindle the Antioch attitude.

"I guess if that has happened it has been our fault," pastor Smith confessed.

"I don't think so; at least not entirely," continued John. "Neither of us has really known how to pull things together in a way that makes Acts 13:1-3 fit us. I don't think we need to say it is anyone's fault—the church, the missionary, or the mission agency. I know that my mission agency has not wanted to supplant the church. But it probably feels it can work more efficiently if it deals with missionaries independently."

Pastor Smith interrupted. "John, I did not even offer you a cup of coffee. It sounds like you are embarking on a pretty long discourse."

While the pastor was preparing the coffee, John walked over to a small chalkboard in the corner of the office. He drew a triangle. On the bottom left angle he wrote "local church"; then on the right, "mission agency." On the top where the triangle came to a point he wrote "missionary." Under "local church" he wrote, "spiritual accountability." Under "mission agency" he put the words "organizational accountability."

Missionary

Three-Way Partnership

Local Church
(Spiritual Accountability)

Mission Agency
(Organizational Accountability)

"Say, John, you *have* been doing some thinking," said Pastor Smith, glancing up as he poured the coffee.

"Well I can't deny that," responded John. "Sometimes I wonder where all this thinking is taking me. I must admit, though, that this simple triangle was a breakthrough for me in trying to understand my relationship to my church and my mission agency. Trying to work some of these things out in real life is going to be a challenge, but they are becoming much clearer.

"It seems obvious to me that when the Holy Spirit called Saul and Barnabas into missions, a partnership between three distinct entities resulted: the *church* at Antioch, the *missionary team* (the closest thing we have to an agency), and of course the individual *missionary*. If we try to apply that to us, we would say that effectiveness in missions depends on just how well those three entities relate to each other.

"You see, the missionary is accountable both to the church and his mission team, or putting it into our context, to the mission agency. But this accountability is not the same in each case. The accountability is defined both by the nature of church and the nature of the mission agency."

"You will have to explain that, John," said the pastor.

"Let me try," John responded. "The church is a spiritual family. The accountability of the missionary to the church is basically *spiritual*. However, the church releases the missionary to a missionary agency, which is an organization. You might say the church delegates *organizational* accountability of the missionary to the agency."

"I understand your words," replied Pastor Smith. "But tell me how this works out in everyday life."

"Well, I guess you could say that the mission agency has an *administrative* responsibility to the missionary, whereas the church's role is primarily to provide a *shepherding* ministry. When roles are reversed, neither the church nor the agency is able to function properly. Churches who get into the management mode with their missionaries pay a high price in the loss of a shepherding relationship. Agencies that fail to administer pay for this neglect in organizational confusion.

"If both the church and the agency really understand their roles, it can result in a beautiful relationship. Biblically, the church recruits

the missionary and equips him spiritually for the ministry to which
God is calling him. The church then usually delegates further training
to the mission agency to prepare the missionary for the assignment
given him. When problems arise the mission might have to make
some tough organizational decisions, but the church should work
with the agency to provide the pastoral ministry of counseling."

Pastor Smith raised his hand, indicating that he needed a break.
"John, you are going too fast. I feel like you have dumped a whole
truckload on me. You need to write these things down so I can try
to understand them. One thing I am hearing is that when mission
agencies do what they are supposed to do, it allows many different
churches, with their missionaries, to come together and work as a
team. I guess if each missionary serving on the team felt free to make
his own decisions, or if each reported directly to his home church,
there would be mass confusion. It would make the ministry practically ineffective. For teamwork to become reality, churches have to
delegate administrative authority to the agencies God has raised up."

"Right," said John. "No group of missionaries can function as
a team when each member is immediately accountable only to his
sending church. Churches that require this kind of accountability
usually decrease the effectiveness of their missionary staff rather
than enhancing it.

"When the church tries to enter into a managerial relationship
with the missionary two things can happen. On the one hand the local
church diminishes the ability of the mission team to provide leadership
and accountability, thus reducing the effectiveness of the missionary.
On the other hand the church compromises its spiritual role and is less
able to encourage, counsel, and "kindle afresh the gift of God" which
was given them through the laying on of hands (2 Tim. 1:6, NASB).

"Churches that insist on exercising immediate organizational
authority over the missionary can create immeasurable confusion
in a missionary team. They can cause suffering in the lives of sin-
cere missionaries who are sensitive about lines of accountability.
On the other side of the coin they can become a tool for missionaries who have a streak of independence and use the church as an
excuse for insubordinate attitudes in the team.

"But though the church delegates organizational *authority* to the agency, it must never shirk its spiritual *responsibility*. The missionary is sent into the field of battle, and his head must be covered with prayer. The church should not only be praying for the missionary; its leadership should encourage its ambassadors to moral purity, healthy relationships, and faithfulness in the ministry. The church has a ministry of keeping the vision of the missionary clear and focused.

"You see," continued John, "in this three-way partnership the missionary is accountable both to the church and the agency. At first this seems impossible, for as is often said, no one can have two bosses. But when both the church and the agency become comfortable with their respective identity and their ensuing roles and responsibilities, this dual accountability becomes a natural expectation on the part of the missionary.

"Pastor, can you imagine how our effectiveness would be enhanced if we could somehow foster genuine teamwork between our church and my mission agency?"

Pastor Smith was again silent. This was heavy stuff, and it would take him time to assimilate it. "John, I think you have become completely idealistic. I doubt whether this could happen in real life. I cannot imagine a missionary agency being able to keep in contact with all the churches represented by their missionaries."

"You're right," John replied. Without communication this is nothing but talk. And you are right about the impossibility of mission agencies keeping in contact with all the churches their missionaries are involved in.

"But Pastor, I can guarantee that it will work with our church if you are willing to do what I will suggest."

"What's that?"

"It will work if *you* take the initiative for the communication."

"What do you mean by that?"

"I mean that the people who are responsible for my mission agency would be delighted to have positive communication from the pastors of the missionaries. Probably the only time they have ever heard from any of them is when there is a complaint.

"Let's try it."

Chapter Eleven

A NEW PERSPECTIVE

Before leaving the restaurant Pastor Smith had pinned down some possible dates for an overnight retreat with several of the church's leaders. It was evident that he was taking these things seriously. He knew, though, that he would have to get the influential members of the church together as soon as possible. The confusion caused by John's message on divorce had provoked quite a bit of discussion among the people.

Arrangements for the retreat were made quickly, and soon John found himself in Pastor Smith's van driving to the retreat center.

The meeting place was well-chosen—a lodge in a nearby state park where they would be able to spend quality time both with the Lord and with each other. The leadership council of the church included not only the pastor's advisory board but also those responsible for the various church ministries. "Leave your cell phones at home," requested Pastor Smith. "If there is an emergency they can call the lodge."

Dinner at the lodge was a time of warm fellowship, mingled with some perplexity. Not everyone was fully aware of what was going to happen during the retreat, though the pastor had tried to prepare them. When they gathered around the fireplace after dinner, however, they all sensed the seriousness of their encounter. The pastor announced that prayer would be integrated into the schedule throughout the retreat. "After each of our encounters we will take time to scatter, either alone or by twos or threes, to offer our discussions to the Lord and seek clarity from His Spirit."

John, of course, led the discussions. He opened his Bible to the book of Esther and read the words of Mordecai in Esther 4: 14: "Who knows whether you have come to the kingdom for such a time as this" (NKJV).

"I don't want to sound too dramatic," began John, "but those of us sitting here have the privilege of being brought into God's spiritual kingdom in what is without doubt one of the most significant periods of all history with respect to the church's mission in the world. There is more prayer for global evangelism than ever before. There is more concerted effort to reach the unreached peoples of the world than ever before. We are living in the period when the gospel is spreading more than ever before.

"The Spirit of God is moving across our globe in an exceptional way, especially in parts of the world where the message of the gospel is penetrating for the first time. Jesus compared the Spirit to wind, which blows where it wishes without anyone knowing where it comes from or where it is going. It is exciting that churches like ours all over the world are hoisting their sails and catching the wind of the Spirit. They are becoming a part of God's movement and finding new life.

The people's expressions told John he was making his point.

"I really love our church, and the greatest tragedy I can imagine would be for her to be tied to the dock during these significant times. Some of you might be thinking that we are too small to play a significant role in God's kingdom. Let me tell you something. The potential of a church is not measured by the number of people who come to the worship, or by its program, or by its building. It is measured by its *vision.*" Again John silently thanked God for the insight he received in his meetings with his friends in Africa.

"I am convinced that in these significant times God is choosing His team—a team of churches anywhere in the world, no matter how insignificant they may seem—that are able to rise to the significance of the times. We could call these churches *World Mission Churches*—churches with three-fold vision."

"Three-fold vision?" asked Pastor Smith, expressing the question mirrored on the faces of the group.

"Let me try to explain," responded John.

"They are churches who have a vision of the *world*. By this I mean they are able to see the world through Acts 1:8." John shared the concept that Acts 1:8 was like a prism, breaking down the world into four parts. He explained that Jesus was using geographical terms as metaphors to define the four great people groups that every church must target in order to be a world church. When he made his point Rick, who was in charge of youth in the church, broke in.

"I always thought that missions meant sending someone to another country, and that reaching people near us was evangelism. Are you saying the two are the same?"

"Yes and no," responded John. "What I am saying is that the world to which the Lord is sending us is the man across the street as well as the man across the globe. When Jesus said that we were to be witnesses in the entire world, He was referring to the world of people, wherever they are found. The people of Jerusalem are the people we can reach out to without leaving home. Those of Judea are people of our own culture, but who live further away. 'Samaritans' refers to people of other cultures living among us. Then of course 'the ends of the earth'

Our Jerusalem—*the people we can reach out to without leaving home*

Our Judea—*the people of our own culture, but who live further away*

Our Samaria—*the people of other cultures living among us*

"The ends of the earth"—*far-away peoples of other cultures and languages*

represent far-away peoples of other cultures and languages. To have global vision means seeing that we should have a *simultaneous* witness to each of these people groups.

"But we are getting ahead of ourselves. World Mission Churches are churches that have a vision of their *mission*. If we are ambassadors for the Lord, then our church is an *embassy*. World Mission Churches not only see the world; they see their responsibility to the world. They understand that the church is missionary by her very nature; she is in the world on mission. They realize that the Great Commission is not merely a command imposed upon the church, but the expression of the very life principle of the church. They know that the coming of the Holy Spirit resulted in an organic union of church and mission."

Harry, the chairman of the deacon board, spoke up. "I have a question. I notice that sometimes you guys...excuse me, I mean you and the pastor, talk about missions, and then you say 'mission.' I can't seem to understand the difference."

"Glad you brought it up," replied John. "The answer is probably easier than you think. The church as a whole has a mission, to make disciples of all nations. Further, in God's plan every local church has a particular mission, and this is what we are going to be grappling with tomorrow. When we are committed to *mission,* then we can start talking about *missions. Missions represent whatever we do to fulfill our mission.*

> Since the church is in the world on mission, and *the church is the people*—then the people are in the world to be on mission.

"But let me finish," John said. "World Mission Churches also have a vision for the church's *potential*.

"Pastor, I am going to say some things that might hurt if you take them personally, but what I am about to say probably describes nine churches out of ten, at least in our country. The tragedy of the majority of the churches is that the people come faithfully every Sunday and occupy a place on the pew, but never realize they are to be on mission. Since the church is in the world on mission, and *the church is the people*—then the people are in the world to be on mission. I know, Pastor Smith, that you realize the meaning of Ephesians 4 where Paul teaches that your job is to equip the saints for the work of the ministry. Somehow, however, because of the divorce between the church and the Great Commission, we just do not associate ministry with missions. If the work of the ministry is directly related to our mission, and it certainly is, then Pastor, your job and mine are the same—to mobilize the people of our church for the church's mission. And to do this we must be able to see their potential."

There was a long silence and the group began to feel the import of John's words. If they had come to the retreat thinking John was going to give them some tips about how they could get involved in *his* ministry, they were mistaken. As they scattered for prayer, they were beginning to get the idea that missions was *their* ministry, and that it was time to get serious about it.

⌇Chapter Twelve⌇

POINTS OF LIGHT

As the men and women of the leadership council gathered after breakfast the following day it was evident the members were both spiritually and physically refreshed, even though it was late the night before when some of them finally went to their rooms. They had taken seriously the admonition to use the remainder of the evening in prayer. Some had gathered in small groups in the lodge while others wandered off alone to seek the face of the Lord. It was apparent that no one wanted to see his church remain tied to the dock when the winds of the Spirit were blowing.

John set up his equipment for a PowerPoint presentation. "Last night we talked about vision," he began after their devotional time. "Clear vision requires focus. Sometimes, when we are really out of focus, we need to wear eyeglasses. I am going to ask all of you to put on a pair of glasses, in the form of a statement. It will be a real help in focusing your vision."

On the screen, in bright yellow letters against a blue background, were these words: "Missions is not what the church does *for* the missionary but what the church does *through* the missionary."

John explained that the small change in prepositions resulted in an entirely new paradigm, a new way of seeing the church and its mission to the world.

"If the church is missionary by her very nature, if the Great Commission is her fundamental law of existence, if Pentecost represents an organic union between the church and her mission—then the church is going to have to be proactive. We have been passive too long. This does not mean that we want to do things independently. We want to be team players with other churches through mission agencies. But we are going to have to take the initiative. "

John asked the group to repeat the slogan several times.

"Let me give you a challenge. This morning I am going to share some thoughts that will outline a course of action for bringing back together what God never meant to be separated. These ideas came from discussions with some of my friends in Africa, and concern how to get our church in S.T.E.P. with the Great Commission. The challenge is to see everything we talk about through this simple slogan. I want you to know it so well that in your sleep you will be saying, 'Missions is not what the church does…'"

Here John stopped, hoping he would hear a strong *"for* the missionary,*"* but there was silence. "Well, we have some work to do," he said, as he continued to work them through the slogan. From time to time during the remainder of the morning he would slip in the first half of the slogan then pause for the response. By the end of the morning the words "for" and "through" became conditioned responses.

All this prompted Sally to state later that John's tactics made her feel like a second grader until, at a certain point during the morning, God opened her eyes and she really started to see things differently. "I guess you knew what you were doing," she admitted.

John spent the remainder of the morning going through the S.T.E.P. process, carefully explaining the value of a Mission Action Plan, the need to put together a team, discussing ways of mobilizing the people of the church, and stressing the importance of linking the church with the outside world through Partners in Prayer. He was encouraged by the apparent ease with which the leadership council grasped the concepts. His daily intercession for his church ever since his meeting with his friends in Africa had made the soil receptive.

By the end of the morning the group was beginning to enjoy the experience of seeing things from a new perspective. The big test came after lunch. They had fun learning the concepts. Now, however, these concepts had to germinate and begin to produce fruit.

"John," said Pastor Smith, "you have emphasized the fact that we need a MAP—a Mission Action Plan, something that will tell us where we are, where we are going, and how to get there. I like the way you say things. Everything is so neat. But those neat little phrases sound almost like a foreign language. I understand the words, but all this is so different from where we live that I would hardly know where to start. You mentioned that our church is like a seed, and that if we do not die by germination we will die by stagnation. This is sobering, and your slogan makes everything sound so simple. But we're not going to change things in our church just by repeating some slogans. In fact, I wonder whether *anything* can ever change in our church."

There was a long pause. The pastor had opened his heart. John knew it was time to leave theory and begin pushing their thinking into just how all this could make a difference in a church like Hillside.

"Thanks, Pastor, for bringing us back to reality. I realize that sometimes I get carried away with ideas."

"Don't take me wrong, John, I am not being critical. Everything starts with ideas. We all have to learn to look at things differently, even when it hurts. The question is—where do we go from here?"

"No matter where we go, there's always a starting point," responded John. "Let's talk about where we are now, or even better, *who* we are. My theory is that the better we understand ourselves, the better we will understand our mission in the world. What are the strengths of our church? What is our potential? In other words, what can we as a church offer to the world?"

Again the silence was long. Pastor Smith struggled with his own thoughts. He wanted to see things in a positive way, but was still smarting from an unkind comment made by one of the church members the week before. It was so much easier to allow his thoughts to slip into the problems people faced him with. He found it hard to muster enough energy to look at those same people as having potential.

Rick started the discussion. "We have some great young people," he volunteered. "Sometimes they get a little bored with what we have to offer them, but if you want to talk about potential, it's there."

"We ought to send some of them over to help John in his work some day. What do you think, John?" This was Mike, a member of the Board of Overseers and a science teacher in the local high school. Somehow no one had ever proposed this before, even though they had heard of other churches sending teams abroad.

"Of course," said John. "As long as we know what they are being sent to do, and we prepare them for it. But let me correct something you just said. If missions is what the church does…"

The missionary is a staff member of the church on assignment in another part of the world.

"*Through* the missionary," was the unanimous reply.

John continued, "Then you would not be sending them over to help in *my* work, but to get involved in *yours*."

"Now even I am beginning to see what you have been trying to say," said Harry. "John, *it is like you are a staff member of the church* on assignment in another part of the world. That means that you are really doing our work. Or, excuse me, that we are doing it through you. Wow."

John knew this was the right time to talk about Partners in Prayer, even though his question about the church's potential was still unanswered. "For the church to fulfill its mission in Africa *through* me means that the church must be involved more than simply sending some young people on a short-term trip. You have to assume ownership of this ministry, just as the church in Antioch did when they laid hands on Saul and Barnabas. And you have to commission someone to be the vital link between the church and me. This is what we mean by a Partner in Prayer."

Mike did not know whether he should speak or keep silent. John's words seemed to light a fire in his heart. Though he did not yet know John well personally, he had admired John ever since coming into the church. Nothing would please him more than to be involved in John's ministry, to realize that he could use his life for something that was making an impact in a part of the world that he could only dream about.

"How about Mike, here," blurted Pastor Smith. "He's about your age, and his kids sure get excited about Africa."

Mike uttered a silent "thank you," responding simply, "it would be my honor." "We'll talk," said John with a strong sense of affirmation.

"Right now, though, we have not made too much progress on our question. Does our church have any distinctive qualities that God could use in global mission—right here in our Jerusalem, reaching out to our Judea and Samaria, and touching the ends of the earth? What are things that strike you about our church?"

"We're just ordinary people," said Sally. "We have our problems, and we have had our ups and downs. But somehow people keep hanging in there. In spite of our problems, people do seem to care for each other. I notice that no one seems to want to go home after services. They hang around in little groups and talk. It's almost like we have little churches in the big church."

In his effort to keep things on track, John was about to allow Sally's remark to go unnoticed, when Harry came alive.

"Maybe *that's* it," he exclaimed, "maybe *that's* what our potential is."

"I don't understand," said John.

"Little churches," continued Harry. "Our church is full of little churches, but we have never recognized them. These little groups are like families; not only do they see each other after church, but you see them together in restaurants. They have a concern for each other. They are probably what holds our church together. John, you mentioned that our church was like a seed that needed to be planted in order to germinate. Maybe we are more like a plant that has produced a lot of little seeds. Maybe this is our main potential.

"It seems to me that if we could get our eyes off ourselves, we could see little groups spring up outside our church as well as inside. Little churches. Little groups of people who care and share. I've noticed that when people visit our church from the outside they often do not come back. But whenever the people of these little groups attract their friends they usually stay with us. If these little groups, the kind we already have, existed in the community they would be like little lighthouses."

"You might be mixing your metaphors a bit," said John. "We've gone from seeds to lighthouses. That's quite a jump."

"But it's a good one. I like the lighthouse idea. Each little group would be a 'Point of Light.'" Pastor Smith was beginning to get excited. Somehow he had seen the little groups as cliques more than little churches. Now he was beginning to see them as a strength. "What if we were to commission some of our little groups to retain their identity but go out into our Jerusalem to be a Point of Light—to care for needs of people around them, to pray with them, to share the Good News through their lives and their words?"

"Not just to our Jerusalem," joined in Mike. "Think of all the people who have left us through the years to live elsewhere. They are scattered all over our Judea. Never once, though, have we seen them as our ambassadors, reproducing Points of Light wherever they went. I wish we could back up and do a commissioning service for each person who has left."

"Don't forget Samaria," said Rick. "Do you realize that our university young people are rubbing shoulders with students from the four corners of the world?"

"Plus the fact that we have a large Hispanic population right here," spoke up Sally. "And I imagine they would appreciate a little care and concern from time to time."

"Well," said John, "who knows where this could take us as a church? You have planted the idea in my own heart. This is something our Bible Institute students in Africa could do. We have been so bound by traditional ideas of church planting that the students think they have to wait until they graduate before they can be involved in church planting."

Before the leadership council members piled into the van to return home, Pastor Smith made this comment. "John, if we could put this into some kind of workable plan, it could turn us outward. As I think about it, though, you were looking for something distinctive about our church. I imagine that what we have identified as our potential would be true of churches all over the place. Why couldn't they do the same thing?"

"They can," replied John, "if someone will teach them how to *see*."

Chapter Thirteen

A WORLD MISSION CHURCH

John's schedule allowed him only four months in the States before he had to return to the institute in Africa. Never before had he experienced so much satisfaction during such a short amount of time. It would take time and patience for these new concepts to work themselves out in Hillside Church. Some people would never get on board, and there would be disappointments. But the biggest change was what had occurred in his own heart.

He realized that he was beginning to see the church differently, as if through new eyes. His past experiences in his church, as well as in raising support, had conditioned him to see the church from the underside, with all its imperfections. In a small way he was starting to sense something of the glory of the church, the masterpiece of the Lord's creative genius. The feeling he was experiencing was somewhat like taking off in a plane in the fog, then breaking through the clouds and seeing the splendor of the sunshine, transforming the gray mist into something of beauty.

The problems were still there, of course, but he was no longer preoccupied with them. The pastors of the churches he visited noticed his excitement. John's new vision was helping them begin to see new potential in *their* people.

John's conversations with the staff of his mission were particularly encouraging. Before John met with its leaders, Pastor Smith had already phoned the agency to ask how the church could best fulfill its part of the team relationship. When John met with the mission director, he learned this was one of the few times a pastor had called the mission for that purpose, although the director had received many problem-related calls. "It took me by surprise," the director said, "and I hardly knew what to say. I can assure you it made me think. In fact, it is moving me to do some new thinking in the whole area of church relationships. We need to talk about these things. I really would like to know what is going on in your church that would prompt your pastor to make that call."

"Maybe we can work together on some of these ideas," replied John, somewhat amused.

One of the greatest encouragements during the four months was the response of the churches to the Partners in Prayer concept as a key means of involving the church in focused prayer. It seemed that the churches were prepared for the idea. "We had been looking for some way to get our people more involved in the ministry in Africa, but somehow our ideas got lost in committees," was the typical response. "This is so practical, and so easy to implement," one pastor exclaimed.

John had recruited a personal Partner in Prayer from each of his supporting churches except three. He knew that some of the relationships he was starting to develop would be deep and long lasting. He also knew that, as the missionary, he would have to take the initiative in establishing good communication, but it would be worth the effort. Now that e-mail was available even where he lived in Africa, he could send brief weekly reports to his partners.

It was his sending church, however, that gave him the greatest satisfaction. The changes that were beginning to occur in the church were remarkable. Hillside Community had started to show evidence of being a church that was turning outward to the world. Of course, not everyone expressed joy about the difference. This was especially true after Pastor Smith's statement that the size of a church is measured by its sending capacity not its seating capacity. In the same message he said that for many years the church had been in the process of dying by stagnation, but now he wanted to see it die by germination, like a seed planted in the ground. As might be expected, some of the pews *were* empty the following week—pews that had been occupied for years by people who enjoyed being watered more than being planted.

During their retreat at the state park, the leadership council had adopted the S.T.E.P. process as a basic plan for reuniting the church with its mission. They had agreed that the main tactic of the church would be to encourage the planting of Points of Light in their Jerusalem, Judea, Samaria, and the ends of the earth. This concept was particularly fascinating to Harry, who had responded so enthusiastically to Sally's remark that their church was comprised of little churches. He was so committed to the idea that he could already see Points of Light nearly everywhere—in their town, at the university with the international students, and in Africa through the students John would send to surrounding villages. Harry's friends knew that when he was captivated by an idea he usually made it happen. They had not seen him so enthusiastic about anything for years.

> The size of a church is measured by its sending capacity not its seating capacity.

Harry had accepted the role of Global Mission Coordinator, and had truly become a right-hand man to the pastor. He was seeing new potential in people, and his training in business administration made him sensitive to the people's capacities. He seemed to know how to get the best out of them without pushing them beyond their limits. The Mission Action Plan he had helped the leadership council put together was brief, simple, and realistic, focused on creating Points of Light both in their city and elsewhere. He had purposely kept the plan free from a lot of policy material, insisting that the main thing was to know where they were going and how to take the next step. He said he wanted things to grow organically, through relationships, rather than organizationally, through structure. Even though most of the folks did not understand what he meant, he had a way of getting them involved.

Harry's immediate task was to work with Pastor Smith in putting together a Global Missions Team. They were agreed that it absolutely must not function as a committee, which means that the people on the team would be handpicked to fulfill specific responsibilities. This meant that the people chosen would have to show both commitment and competence, as well as having good relationships in the church. The team would play the primary role in integrating the spirit of mission into the church as a whole. Then they would mobilize the people for the role each would play.

The idea of the pyramid with its six parts had been just what was needed for Hillside. The pastor's choice of people to fill the positions had been wise. These people were self-starters but not independent. The contrast between mission team meetings and some of the committee meetings of the church was dramatic. The team members knew what they were supposed to do and took their responsibilities seriously. They came to meetings prepared to share what was happening, ask advice, and make sure what they were doing was coordinated with the others. Pastor Smith was amazed at how a sense of ownership unleashes people's potential.

The pastor's messages, new vision through the Mission Action Plan, the enthusiasm of the Global Mission Team, the involvement of an increasing number of members in reaching their community—all this was pumping vitality into the church. Many of the members had begun to feel a new sense of purpose. It was truly a revisiting both of Acts 1:8 and the first sending of a missionary team from Antioch in Acts 13.

John's four months on home ministries were soon gone. Again he found himself having lunch with his pastor. They were discussing John's final message to the church before his departure.

"Do you realize, my dear friend, that Sunday will be the last time you will be in our church before going back to Africa. You really shook us up on your first Sunday. How about something more encouraging this time?"

They both laughed.

Chapter Fourteen

HIS GLORIOUS CHURCH

Two years had passed since John's return to his ministry in Africa. It had been one of the busiest—and most satisfying—periods of his life.

His teaching ministry had undergone a transformation; it happened almost without his being aware of the change. Personalizing Acts 13:1-3 was a starting point not only in relating the Scriptures to his life, but it also became a pattern for teaching others. He realized he had been doing a good job *instructing* his students, but not necessarily *equipping* them for their ministry. Rather than merely *transplanting* biblical knowledge, he was now trying to devote himself to *implanting* truth that would lead to changed values and behavior.

Since being in Africa he had become painfully aware that, though many of the African churches were large and filled with people, their faith was too often based on a narrow layer of biblical knowledge rather than heart-felt obedience to the Word of God. He longed to see Christians living out a genuine biblical culture.

All this required his being an example of what he was teaching, organizing biblical knowledge around the seed truths that were already bearing fruit in his life. It also meant that his students needed to be practicing the truth they were beginning to understand. This required him to spend time with them on weekends as well as in the classroom during the week.

Being with his students on weekends brought him great satisfaction. His heroes in the past had been his teachers in Bible college. Though he admired them, he knew that sometimes their involvement in mission was more theoretical than practical. Unconsciously he had adopted the philosophy that a teacher's ministry was pretty much confined to infusing knowledge into his students, not necessarily becoming personally involved in helping them reach out to people.

It was different now. He understood that if missions in Hillside Community Church was measured by what those people were doing *through* him and not merely *for* him, he carried a great responsibility to them and to the Lord for bearing personal fruit. The very fact that eight faithful Partners in the Great Commission were interceding for him daily, eagerly awaiting his weekly e-mail update, provided a great deal of motivation. For the first time in his ministry he was faithfully keeping a contact book, which he saw as his own personal garden that he was cultivating through prayer and planned encounters. The effect of this simple practice was dramatic, making *people* rather than *projects* his priority.

All this had climaxed just three weeks earlier when a team of five college students, accompanied by Harry, the Global Outreach Coordinator, came to Africa on a short-term mission trip. The class schedule at the Bible Institute had been cleared for two weeks. In the morning the visiting team shared their experiences in reaching out to their own community. They talked about discipleship training leading to Points of Light that they prayed would become new churches. In the afternoon the American visitors joined the African students to minister in established churches and among village people in the surrounding area. The Bible Institute teachers served as interpreters.

This was a new experience for the Africans, and it was bathed in prayer. John's fellow-teachers expressed some skepticism during the planning sessions, and, indeed, they did make some mistakes. But everyone was convinced by the enthusiastic response of the people that God had led in sending this team. The bonding between the Americans and Africans was evident from the start, in spite of the huge cultural gap between them. Several Points of Light were begun, Growth Groups were initiated (something entirely new for the churches), and plans were made for training sessions to be organized by the students.

However, nothing in the memory of Hillside Community Church could compare with the electrifying effect of the return of the team from Africa. When the students stepped off the plane, their parents knew immediately they were greeting sons and daughters who were different from those they had sent away. One of the fathers even expressed some concern to Harry, wondering how long it would take for his son to revert to his normal self. "Maybe what you see now *is* his normal self," responded Harry, not helping the situation at all.

Their testimonies were highlighted for several Sundays. At times their sharing became emotional. One of the young ladies broke down describing the kind of suffering she had not previously known existed on this planet. The people of Hillside realized how deeply their own youth had been impacted by this experience, perhaps not recognizing how they themselves were being impacted. Already plans were underway for sending another team the following year.

One thing was evident. Their missionary John no longer seemed so far away. His life was a part of theirs as never before. Whenever Harry stood before the congregation he never failed to remind them that missions is not what the church does *for* the missionary, but *through* the missionary. He reminded them that Hillside Community had seen God work through their very own children, the young people on the team who in every sense of the word were missionaries sent from the church for a specific mission, which, he added, they fulfilled admirably well.

"But," continued Harry, "don't get the idea that what we did in Africa is all that different from what the Gibsons, or the Arnetts, or the Joneses are doing right in our own town. Or what is happening on the campus. Or the Hispanic group that has begun to meet. Of course the setting between our town and the village where John is working could not be more different. As the young people have said in so many ways, it is almost inconceivable that there can be such a contrast in the living conditions of people living on the same globe. Probably many of you have been moved emotionally from the things we have shared—your hearts go out to these people in their suffering.

"But let's not forget that many of our neighbors are just as needy as anyone we saw during our two weeks in Africa. Yes, they live in beautiful homes, have plenty to eat, and are only minutes away from a modern hospital. But if they do not know the Lord, they are just as lost as anyone in the world whether they live in luxury or misery. The ministry trip to Africa was a great highlight for our church, and you should be extremely proud of your young people and the way they served. As the Global Outreach Coordinator, I want you to know I am just as proud of all of you who are convinced that our mission is to the man across the street as well as around the globe. In fact, in some ways it is even more difficult to remember that they too are our mission, because the people across the street are so much like us."

Harry's remarks were winding up the final Sunday morning of sharing. If Harry felt pride for all the people of Hillside who were awakening to mission, Pastor Smith felt even greater pride for Harry, the man he had appointed to coordinate the global outreach of their church. "This man's wisdom is remarkable," thought the pastor as he sat listening to those words. "The experience of the team was so positive that it could almost have driven a wedge between them and the rest of the people. Instead, Harry has made it a springboard to affirm the people who are doing the very same thing right here in our town."

Pastor Smith tried to concentrate on the remainder of Harry's message, but found it hard. He gave in to the temptation of allowing his thoughts to wander, and increasingly felt himself enveloped in a feeling of warmth and fullness. He reminded himself that he was still Pastor Smith of Hillside Community Church, surrounded by the people whom he had known for years—people for whom he had poured out the best of his life.

Yes, the same church. But was it the same? Sure, he still had to deal with some conflicts. Once in a while people still made statements that hurt. Not all the board meetings were pleasant.

Yet, *was* it the same church? Something had happened, and was continuing to happen. There were problems, to be sure, but now there was a purpose that the people had never known before. A lot of struggles, but potential in the midst of those struggles that gave hope. Disagreement at times on *how* best to do things, but a deepening sense of unity on *what* needed to be done. Concern for local needs, but growing awareness of the crying needs of a world that began at their very doorstep and stretched to the ends of the earth. People were actually beginning to *see* that world. And seeing the world, they were seeing their own significance as God's sent ones—His ambassadors.

Pastor Smith was now experiencing a feeling deep in his soul that he had almost lost in his commitment to the ministry—*life, true spiritual life.* He wanted the feeling to last forever. Was this what John had been trying to explain when he said that the Spirit of the church was the Spirit of mission? Was he actually experiencing what happens when the Spirit of mission is unleashed? Was he—and the church—actually experiencing the fullness of the Spirit, the author of love, joy, peace, and all the qualities that he had tried so hard, and so unsuccessfully, to infuse into the church?

> The Spirit of the church is the Spirit of mission.

Yes, something *had* changed. The very things he had tried so hard to achieve were apparently happening. In a way it seemed too easy. Could this mean that after all these years he was finally allowing Jesus to be the Head of His church, to assume ownership and make it functional? For the church to be the means by which He was completing the ministry that He had begun on the cross?

It was something Pastor Smith had never experienced before. It was almost as if an unseen force was lifting him higher—to a point where he could see the church from above. What he saw was beautiful, more beautiful than he could imagine, totally unlike the church from the underside. It was the church of which he was a part, the church he will know in its fullness when he sits with the Lord at the heavenly marriage feast. It was a glorious church.

With a start Pastor Smith quickly became aware that all eyes were upon him. Harry had finished his message and had taken his seat. Some wondered why Pastor Smith seemed so preoccupied and moved directly to the closing prayer. But the intensity of his prayer left no doubt about the fire burning in his soul.

In one way his Monday morning would be the same as always. Yet in another way his Monday mornings would never be the same. For a brief moment God had pulled back the veil and allowed him to see.

Never again would he would he have to wonder about the meaning of mission.

Reuniting Your Church with Her Mission

A manual to help you bring back together what God meant never to be separated—your church and her worldwide mission

⤜Manual⤏

This manual is an outline of the concepts you encountered
in reading the story of John and his experiences at Hillside
Community Church.

It is provided as a tool to help you implement these concepts—
personally, with your friends, and in your ministry.

Here are three suggestions to help you get the most out of the
manual:

1. Use it personally as a means of reviewing the story
   of John. It will help you focus on the concepts that
   opened his eyes to a new understanding of the church
   and her mission. Highlight the concepts that are
   meaningful to you, and explore ways of implementing
   them in your own ministry.

2. Work through the manual until you are able to develop
   your own personalized plan for reuniting *your* church
   with her mission. This will become a mental map that
   will allow you to plant these concepts in meetings and
   personal conversations as opportunities arise, "making
   the most of every opportunity" (Ephesians 5:16).

3. Use the manual as a syllabus for teaching these concepts to your church leadership team or to the missions
   commission of your church. If you are a missionary,

share these concepts with your missionary team and supporting churches. As preparation, have them read through John's story.

(The answers for filling in the blanks begin on page 116.)

At the beginning of the twenty-first century, we are faced with two great realities.

1. *The times have never been more significant.*
   - There is more prayer for world evangelization in our generation than ever before in the history of the church.
   - There is a greater concerted effort to reach the world in our generation than ever before in the history of the church.
   - More people are coming to Christ in our generation than ever before in the history of the church.

2. *God is bringing together a team of churches that are rising to the challenge of the hour.*
   - These churches have a vision of the **world**, seeing the nations of the world through the prism of Acts 1:8: *Jerusalem* (people of their own culture within their reach), *Judea* (people of their own culture further away), *Samaria* (people of other cultures within their reach), and *the ends of the earth* (people of other cultures further away).
   - These churches have a focus on **mission**, seeing Matthew 28:18-20 as the fundamental law of the existence of the church, and not merely an external command.
   - These churches have a commitment to global **teamwork**, willing to follow the model of Acts 13:1-3 by seeing potential in their people and by releasing them to be a part of God's greater team.

A New Way of Seeing

Missions is not what the church does *for* the missionary, but what the church does *through* the missionary.

On the surface, those two statements seem almost alike. Yet, they express viewpoints that are profoundly different.

The difference is in the way we see.

To move from one concept to the other is like taking off one pair of eyeglasses and putting on another.

IF WE BELIEVE that missions is what the church does **through** *the missionary, it will affect the way we see our* _____.

We will see that our church is in the world to be on mission, not merely to maintain her own existence. This means that our church must take initiative by being *proactive* in the fulfillment of the Great Commission, not just by *reacting* to appeals by missionaries. As was true of the church of Antioch, missions must grow out of our church, rather than being grafted on. This is more than being merely "missions-minded."

IF WE BELIEVE that missions is what the church does **through** *the missionary, it will affect the way we see our* _____.

We will see that the mission of our church is not merely to support missionaries, but to make disciples of all nations and gather them together into spiritual families. This means entering into a caring relationship with nations through adoption of people groups. When new churches are born, we will see them as a part of our extended spiritual family with whom we have a relationship and responsibility.

IF WE BELIEVE that missions is what the church does **through** *the missionary, it will affect the way we see our* _____.

We will see that our missionaries are not merely outsiders who come occasionally to share about *their* work in order to gain financial support. We will see them as members of our staff, doing *our* work, members of our global team and vital links between our church and the nations of the world for fulfilling our church's mission. We will see mission agencies as partners in the Great Commission, serving our churches by allowing us to do together what we could not do alone.

Part I: The Great Divorce

The Gospel of Matthew records two encounters that have profound implications for missions.

Matthew 16:18-19, "The Great _____"

Matthew 28:18-20, "The Great _____"

These two encounters represent two streams in divine revelation that flowed together on the day of Pentecost. Yet, through the centuries churches have become divorced from their mission. *Our task is to bring back together what God intended never to be separated.*

A. The Great Prediction, Matthew 16:18-19

The main clause: *"I will build my church."*

The subordinate clauses:
   "The gates of Hades shall not overpower it."
   "I will give you the keys of the kingdom of heaven."
   "Whatever you shall bind on earth shall be bound in heaven."

1. Principle: The church is missionary by nature.

   a. The church is _____, a body of called out ones.

      Only as she continues to call out can she continue to exist as church.

   b. The church is the _____ of Christ.

      The church, as a second, spiritual incarnation, is the means by which Christ is *proclaiming* the salvation that He *procured* in His first incarnation.

   c. The church will be _____ by Christ.

      As the Spirit of Christ, the *paraklete* (the One who

comes alongside to call), summons a people for His name, the church is built.

2. Application: The church is given a three-fold mission.

   a. The church is to _____ against the gates of Hades.

      "Gates of Hades" refers to the principalities and powers of the unseen world. The church is to invade the world, the domain of the prince of darkness.

   b. The church is given the _____ of the Kingdom of heaven.

      The church is to deliver people from the domain of darkness and open the door to the kingdom of our Lord.

   c. The church is given the ministry of _____ and _____.

      The church is to bind those who are loosed from the kingdom of this world into the fellowship of the believers (Matthew 18:18).

B. The Great Commission, Matthew 28:18-20

The main clause: *"Make disciples of all the nations."*

The subordinate clauses:
   "Go, therefore."
   "Baptizing them in the name of the Father, and the Son, and the Holy Spirit."
   "Teaching them to observe all that I commanded you."

1. Principle: The Great Commission is the fundamental law of existence for the church.

   a. It is given by _____

God's plan is to bring together under one head all things both in heaven and in earth (Ephesians 1: 9-10). The church is the focal point of God's plan (Ephesians 1:22).

b. It is given to _____

The church is built on the foundation of the Apostles and Prophets (Ephesians 2:20). Though the Great Commission applies individually to every Christian, the solemn setting of Matthew 28:18-20 requires us to see it as a formal purpose statement to the divinely chosen representatives of the corporate body.

c. It is a statement of _____

Though the church has many purposes, such as worship, fellowship and edification, she has one primary earthly mission—to make disciples. This can be done only as local churches reproduce themselves throughout the world.

The Great Commission is the life principle of the church. It is a law of existence and not merely an external command.

Mission flows from the essential nature of the church. It is a part of the church's DNA. Neglect of the Great Commission will render the church dysfunctional.

2. Application: the Great Commission expresses the three-fold mission of the church.

a. The church is to make disciples by _____.

The church, covered with divine authority, is to penetrate the domain of the "gates of Hades," and to prevail.

b. The church is to make disciples by _____.

Baptism, as the public confession of Christ, is the outward sign both to men and angels of a disciple's entrance into the kingdom of heaven.

   c. The church is to make disciples by _____

everything that Jesus taught.

Obedience to Christ's commands binds disciples into the fellowship of the believers.

Note the parallelism between the Great Prediction and the Great Commission.

C. The Great Divorce

1. The Organic Union of the Church with her Mission (Acts 1:8)

Two main clauses:

> *"You shall receive power when the Spirit has come upon you."*
> *"You shall be my witnesses."*

  a. Principle: The coming of the Spirit produced an organic union between the church and her mission.

When the Spirit of Jesus descended upon the believers, the church was born as a living organism.

The first act of the newborn church was to spill out into the streets of Jerusalem on mission.

From that time on, the story of the New Testament is how the disciples wove together the church and the Great Commission into the fabric of their ministries.

  b. Application

    1) The Spirit of Christ is the Spirit of the church.

      • The Holy Spirit is the Spirit of _____.

Pentecost is the union of Christ with His disciples through the Spirit.

(Matthew 28:20, John 14:28, Colossians 1:27)

The _____ is the result of the union of Christ with His disciples.

The church is not an organization, but a living organism. (1 Corinthians 12:13)

- The church becomes the _____ of Christ.

The purpose of the body is to fulfill the desires of the head. (Ephesians 1:22-23)

2)   The Spirit of Christ is the Spirit of mission.

- The Holy Spirit supplies the _____ needed by the disciples to prevail against the gates of Hades (Acts 1:8).

Though Satan has been stripped of his authority (Colossians 2:15), he still exercises great power.

- The Holy Spirit _____ people of sin, righteousness and judgment. (John 16:7-11)

Only those convicted of their need will enter into the kingdom of God.

- The Holy Spirit _____ people together as members of the body of Christ. (1 Corinthians 12:27)

Through the unity of the Spirit, the church is bound together as a functioning body, not gathered together as a collection of body parts (Ephesians 4:3-4).

3)   There is only one Spirit.

He is the *paraklete.*

- He is the one who *comes alongside (para)*, making us a part of the church. (Romans 8:9)

- He is the one who *calls (kaleo)*, making us ambassadors of Christ. (2 Corinthians 5:20)

To quench the Spirit of mission is to quench

the only Spirit that exists.

Because the church is *ekklesia* and missionary by nature…

Because the Great Commission is the fundamental law of existence of the church…

Because the Holy Spirit brought about an organic union between the church and her mission…*your church is in the world on mission.*

2. The Divorce

  a. The background

  In the beginning, there was an organic union between the church and her mission in the world.

  You cannot understand the church without seeing it through the Great Commission. Further, you cannot understand the Great Commission without seeing it through the church.

  Yet, over time, they separated.

  When the church forgot her heavenly citizenship in order to pursue an earthly kingdom, she lost sight of her divine mission. The world became her *parish*, rather than her *mission field*.

  As heirs of this historic distortion, we have created two compartments in our thinking, putting the church in one and missions in the other.

  b. The results of this divorce are sadly evident.

   1) The Autonomy of Missions

   With respect to the _____: many missionaries are spiritual orphans with little or no relationship to their churches.

   With respect to the _____: many

mission agencies operate independently of the churches that support them, allowing almost anything to be considered missionary work.

With respect to _____: culture has often supplanted the church as the reference point for mission philosophy.

2) The Impoverishment of the Church

With respect to its _____: when a church turns inward it risks becoming self-centered and provincial.

With respect to its _____: when a church focuses on its own needs it risks becoming materialistic.

With respect to its _____: when a church neglects its worldwide mission the Spirit is quenched, resulting in carnality.

When the Great Commission is taken out of the church, that church risks becoming nothing more than an ecclesiastical institution.

When the church is taken out of the Great Commission, missions risks becoming nothing more than evangelistic or social activism.

Part II: Getting your Church in S.T.E.P. with the Great Commission

This section introduces the S.T.E.P. process, one way your church can bring together what God intended never to separate: church and mission.

Phase One of S.T.E.P.

Strategy: Formulating a Mission Action Plan

A. What is a Mission Action Plan (MAP)?

A Mission Action Plan is a statement of _____ and how to reach them.

1. *A Mission Action Plan is a MAP. Like any map, the Mission Action Plan answers three questions:*

    • _____

    • _____

    • _____

2. *A Mission Action Plan causes us to focus on goals.*

    • Goals provide_____

    • Goals give_____

    • Goals permit_____

    • Goals measure_____

A goal is something you aim for, not necessarily something you hit.

B. What does a Mission Action Plan do?

1. A Mission Action Plan takes us out of the _____ mode and into the _____ mode.

   A MAP will get the church moving. Once it is moving, a church can then change direction if necessary.

2. A Mission Action Plan gives us context for making _____.

   In most churches the mission program evolves through reaction to appeals rather than through prayerful planning. A church without a MAP is vulnerable to emotional appeals.

3. A Mission Action Plan opens our eyes to our _____.

   If we do not have a plan it is impossible to see where people fit in.

C. Preparing a Mission Action Plan

Biblical planning should be "inside out" rather than "outside in." That is, all planning begins with the church's resources and present commitments rather than with an imposed program.

1. Where are we?

   The first step in the preparation of a Mission Action Plan is an evaluation of the church's present status. Present involvement is the springboard for effective planning for the future.

   This is the _____ stage of planning.

   This information should be summarized into a profile of the church's resources, commitment to the Great Commission, and opportunities.

   This profile becomes the basis for planning.

Three research questions:

- What strengths and resources of our church can be dedicated to our Acts 1:8 mission?

- What is our present involvement in Acts 1:8 ministries?

  What are the nations and people groups with whom we have been involved during the past ten years? What is our current involvement?

  Who are the missionaries we have sent out during the past ten years? Who are we currently sending?

  What churches have we helped plant in the last ten years? What churches are we currently helping to plant?

- What are the open doors of Acts 1:8 that the Lord has set before us?

2. Where are we going?

   This is the _____ aspect of planning. Vision is our perception of what we believe our mission to be. It is painting a picture for the future. This picture should be reduced to specific goals.

   The members of the Global Mission Team should schedule a minimum of one full day in a retreat setting, along with the pastor and other members of the church leadership. Time should be given to evaluating the profile of the present involvement of the church, praying for guidance, and dreaming into the future.

   The retreat should focus on three areas: adopting people groups, mobilizing missionaries, and planting churches.

   Three vision questions:

   - What people groups are we committed to reaching in our Acts 1:8 mission?

   - What missionaries are we committed to sending in our Acts 1:8 mission?

- What church-planting projects are we committed to in our Acts 1:8 mission?

3. How do we get there?

   This is the _____aspect of planning.

   The answer to where the church is going should produce a list of goals that will give direction to its global mission. The definition of goals, however, is not a guarantee that they will be met. The Global Missions Team must now formulate action steps for each goal and assign these to responsible people.

   Three action questions:

   - What is the next step for each goal?

   - Who is responsible to take the next step? To whom is he or she accountable?

   - When should the next step be taken?

   Planning is hard work. Planning is not to be confused with policy-making. Policy establishes the boundaries; planning identifies the goals. Policy tells us what we can do and what we cannot do; planning tells us where we are going. Policy refers to performance and is easy to formulate. Planning refers to direction and demands a much higher level of commitment and personal responsibility. It is easy to stay in bounds; it is harder to achieve goals.

Phase Two of S.T.E.P.

Teamwork: Recruiting a Global Missions Team

A. Mobilizing a Team

The prerequisite for the implementation of the S.T.E.P. process is the mobilization of a *team* of committed and qualified people. In some churches this team coordinates all the

Acts 1:8 ministries of the church, including local outreach. In others, the team specializes in overseas ministries.

1. A team is not a committee.

   - In a _____, the members are often chosen without being given any defined responsibility. The main function of the member is to respond to the leader's proposals, and the leader leads by consensus.

   - In a _____ the members are handpicked because of their commitment and ability. Each team member has a defined responsibility. The role of the member is to report and coordinate. The leader gives direction to the team.

2. The characteristics of a team.

   - It has defined goals
   - The members have defined roles
   - It has a leader who coordinates

B. Building a Global Mission Pyramid

No matter how large or small your church, you will need to fill six functions in order to implement the S.T.E.P. process and effectively reunite your church with her mission: direction, organization, communication, intercession, provision, mobilization.

These six functions can be illustrated by a pyramid. The pyramid has three levels: the top level gives direction, the middle level supplies coordination, and the bottom level brings mobilization.

1. The point of the pyramid: direction

    a. The_____ _____
        is the key person on the Global Missions Team.

        This must be a person with clear vision, good
        organizational experience, and strong relational skills.

    b. *Responsibilities:*

        •   To handpick members and supervise the ministry
            of the Global Mission Team.

        •   To master the S.T.E.P. process.

        •   To direct the formulation and implementation of
            a Mission Action Plan.

        •   To coordinate the formulation and
            implementation of a program for mission
            mobilization.

        •   To serve as the link between the church and
            mission agencies.

        •   To report regularly to the leadership of the
            church.

2. The base of the pyramid: praying, giving, and going

   The mobilization of the people of the church will focus on three areas: intercession, giving, and going. A competent and dedicated member of the team must coordinate each of these three areas.

   • _____   _____

   Purpose: To assure that the members of the church are mobilized for intercession for the mission of the church.

   Responsibilities: Mobilize the church in prayer for the calling of missionaries. Oversee the flow of information from the outreach ministries to the church. Coordinate the ministry of the Partners in the Great Commission. Attend the prayer groups regularly to evaluate their effectiveness. Integrate prayer for mission into the public ministries of the church.

   Qualifications: An understanding of the indispensable nature of prayer, a deep commitment to prayer, and strong relational and organizational skills.

   • _____   _____

   Purpose: To assure that the financial needs of the Mission Action Plan are cared for in the most effective way.

   Responsibilities: Examine and evaluate the financial needs of the outreach ministries of the church. Partner with missionary staff in support raising. Evaluate accounting procedures of the church. Counsel individuals concerning giving.

   Qualifications: Knowledge of finances and a biblical philosophy of giving; concern for the financial needs of missionaries.

   • _____   _____

   Purpose: To discern the giftedness and calling of those whom God is choosing and challenge them toward recruitment into the mission ministries of the church.

Responsibilities: Understand thoroughly the Mission Action Plan. Evaluate the human resources of the church in light of the needs of the strategy. Challenge and recruit for all aspects of missionary involvement.

Qualifications: A commitment to the mission strategy of the church, strong relational skills, and active involvement in church ministries.

3. The bonding of the pyramid: organization and communication

   • _____ _____

   Purpose: Take responsibility for the organization of all activities related to the Mission Action Plan.

   Responsibilities: Keep the calendar for all events related to the global outreach of the church. Coordinate visits of missionaries and organize hospitality. Schedule meetings for the missionaries who visit. Organize all functions related to missions, including the missionary conference.

   Qualifications: Organizational and relational skills, commitment, and faithfulness.

   • _____ _____

   Purpose: Infuse the vision and strategy of the church into all aspects of the church's ministry.

   Responsibilities: Develop and implement a plan of education for the entire church, targeting all age groups. Creatively keep the Mission Action Plan before the church. Assure that lines of communication are open on all levels.

   Qualifications: Skills and training in education, active role in the life of the church, concern for people.

Phase Three of S.T.E.P.
Enlisting: Mobilizing Missionaries

A missionary is not necessarily someone who goes from one country to another.

A missionary is someone who is sent from the church into the world.

A missionary is someone commissioned by the church to fulfill a specific mission outside the scope of the existing church.

- A missionary can be anyone in the church, regardless of his or her level of training or position.

- A missionary can be someone sent to any of the four people groups of Acts 1:8.

- A missionary can be commissioned for any period of time.

Just as is true when a country goes to war, all the members of the church should be challenged to feel ownership for the church's mission, and to form a team with the missionaries. This is total mobilization.

A. How missionaries are mobilized

The example of the church in Antioch for the identification and commissioning of missionaries. (Acts 13:1-3)

1. The _____ provided the context for the setting apart of missionaries.

    Paul and Barnabas were already active in the ministry of the church at Antioch. According to Ephesians 4, God gives apostles (in the broad sense, missionaries) to the church.

2. _____ and _____ provided

the context for the missionary call.

3. The church assumed _____ through the laying on of hands, but_____ them as an autonomous team.

4. The church at Antioch continued in _____ with the missionary team.

The entire church should be educated in the Mission Action Plan, through the preaching and teaching ministry of the church, through small group ministries, and through special efforts such as an annual Missions Festival.

Ministry trips, whether local or global, are indispensable in exposing church members to the peoples of the world. (See John 4:35.)

B. Missionaries who are called and qualified should be _____ by the church.

1. Commissioning is a recognition of the divine call of the missionary.

2. Commissioning is a commitment to participation in the ministry of the missionary through prayer and giving.

3. Commissioning is a recognition of the accountability of the missionary to the church.

C. Missionaries are to be _____ by the church to their missionary team.

1. When a missionary is sent, a three-way partnership is established involving the church, the missionary, and the mission team, usually represented by a mission agency.

   a. The main purpose of a mission agency is to ensure teamwork between churches who send and missionaries who are sent.

b. Though the church maintains a shepherding relationship with the missionary, it releases the missionary to the mission team in an organizational relationship.

2. Teamwork between churches and mission teams depends upon a clear definition of roles.

Phase Four of S.T.E.P.
Prayer: Commissioning Partners

The most effective way of building a foundation of prayer for missions is through commissioning a Partner in Prayer for each missionary.

Imagine a power plant capable of generating electricity for hundreds of homes. Imagine these homes equipped with all kinds of electrical appliances. Imagine the engineer forgetting to construct power lines between the plant and the houses. This gives you a picture of many churches and their missionary teams.

The Partner in Prayer is the _____ *between the church and the missionary.*

Biblical example: Epaphroditus (Philippians 2:25)

A. How the Partner in Prayer should be selected.

The selection and appointment of the Partner in Prayer should be a three-way agreement among the _____, the _____, and the _____.

Only one partner (or couple) should be appointed for each missionary.

Chinese proverb: "When two people feed the same mule, the mule dies of hunger." Discuss how this may apply.

The Partner in Prayer should be commissioned publicly so that he is identified as the link with the missionary.

B. The responsibilities of a Partner in Prayer.

- Become acquainted with the yearly ministry goals of the missionary.

- Maintain monthly communication with the missionary by telephone or e-mail, seeking the following information: outstanding blessing, outstanding needs information about ministry (conversions, baptisms, monthly attendance at branch church), progress on goals, family concerns.

- Communicate this information to the leaders of the church (pastor, Great Commission Coordinator, president of the women's group, leaders of other relevant groups.)

- Lead a monthly prayer group for the missionary.

- Meet quarterly with the Great Commission Coordinator and the other Partners in Prayer to evaluate effectiveness.

- Plan, if possible, to visit the missionary on the field every four years.

Part III: Becoming a World Mission Church

A World Mission Church is a church that has:

- *A vision of the* _____

- *A focus on* _____

- *A commitment to* _____

A. A Vision of the World.

The size of a church is not measured by its membership, attendance, facilities, or programs. It is measured by its potential. The potential of these churches will be determined by their vision of what God is doing and their willingness to be a part.

Paul prayed in Ephesians 1:18 that the eyes of the heart might be enlightened. Yet light cannot bring sight unless we are willing to open our eyes to the world and what God is doing in it.

Vision is the result of looking, not at those things that are physically visible, but at those things which are eternal (2 Corinthians 4:18).

1. Vision is the ability to see the significance of the times (Matthew 16:3).

    We live in the most significant period of human history with respect to the calling out of the Bride of our Lord.

2. Vision is the ability to discern the movement of the Spirit (Acts 16:6-10).

When we open the door to the Lord, He opens the door to the world (Revelation 3:20; 3:7).

3. Vision is the ability to focus on people (John 4:31-35).

   The disciples had lost perspective. In this story, the picnic had become more important than the Samaritan woman. Jesus told them to lift up their eyes and look.

B. A Focus on Mission.

The church has many purposes, but only one earthly mission.

1. Like a seed, the church must be _____.

   The characteristics of a seed:

   _____

   _____

   _____

2. The seed must _____ (John 12:24).

   Death is not the extinction of life, but separation from the protective envelope.

   Every church faces death either by _____ or by _____.

3. Through death, the church becomes a _____ _____ plant, not a _____ _____.

C. A Commitment to Teamwork

1. Churches tend to fall into one of two extremes with respect to their responsibility to the mission agency.

- _____

- _____

2. Teamwork between churches and agencies depends upon
    a clear definition of roles.

    The church as an organism must assume *spiritual
    responsibility* for the missionary. This includes prayer,
    recruitment, commissioning, support, communication,
    and shepherding.

    The mission agency as an organization must accept
    organizational authority for the missionary. This includes
    training, assignment, organizational accountability,
    strategy, and policies.

    The missionary has dual accountability:

    _____ to his or her supporting
    church, as a member of the staff.

    _____ to the mission agency,
    as an employee.

Missionary

**Three-Way
Partnership**

Local Church
(Spiritual Accountability)

Mission Agency
(Organizational Accountability)

A final word

Your ability to reunite the church with her mission will be directly related to your vision of the glory of the church.

- The church is the focal point of God's great plan of bringing together all things under the headship of Jesus Christ, Ephesians 1:9-10, 22-23.
- The church is the means by which God is revealing His manifold wisdom, Ephesians 3:10-11.
- The church is the object of the eternal affection of the Lord, Ephesians 5:25-27.

Now to him who is able to do immeasurably more than all we ask or imagine, according to his power that is at work within us, to him be glory in the church and in Christ Jesus throughout all generations, for ever and ever! Amen (Ephesians 3:20-21, NIV).

Never forget...

Missions is not what the church does *for* the missionary, but what the church does *through* the missionary.

CHECK LIST
World Mission Church

Strategy

1. Our church has an up-to-date missions profile, giving our people an adequate understanding of our current global mission involvement

2. Our church has a MAP (Mission Action Plan) with defined goals and action steps.

3. Our church has a program of education integrating the vision and goals of our global mission into all ages and ministries of the church.

Teamwork

4. Our church has a dedicated Great Commission Coordinator.

5. Our church has a functioning Global Missions Team with specific responsibilities for each member.

6. Our church has a program of enlisting and actively mobilizing her members and resources for effective implementation of the Mission Action Plan.

Enlisting

7. Our church recognizes as missionaries anyone who is sent from the church to fulfill a specific mission for any amount of time.

8. Our church publicly commissions all who are sent from the church on mission.

9. Our church seeks to mobilize all its members to participate in its global outreach ministries.

Prayer

10. Our church has commissioned a Partner in Prayer for each of our missionaries.

11. Our church has a specific prayer group for each of its missionaries, led by the Great Commission Partner.

12. Our church integrates prayer for her global mission into the total prayer ministry of the church.

Answer Sheet

Page 90
Church
Mission
Missionary

Page 91
Prediction
Commission
Ekklesia
Body
Built

Page 92
Prevail
Keys
Binding, loosing
The Head of the church

Page 93
The formal representatives
    of the church
The mission of the church
Going
Baptizing

Page 94
Obeying
Jesus
Church

Page 95
Body
Power
Convicts
Binds

Page 96
Missionary
Agency

Page 97
Missiology
Vision
Values
Vitality

Page 98
Goals
Where are we?
Where are we going?
How do we get there?
Direction
Motivation
Teamwork
Progress

Page 99
Maintenance
Mission
Maintenance
Mission
Decisions
Resources
Research

Page 100
Vision

Page 101
Action

Page 102

Committee
Team

Page 103

Global Mission Coordinator

Page 104

Prayer Coordinator
Financial Coordinator
Mission Mobilizer

Page 105

Program Coordinator
Mission Educator

Page 106

Church
Prayer and fasting

Page 107

Responsibility
Released
Partnership
Commissioned
Released

Page 108

Link
Church, Missionary, Partner

Page 110

World
Mission
Teamwork

Page 111

Planted
Life
Purpose
Ability to reproduce
Die
Stagnation, Germination
Seed Bearing, Storage Bin

Page 112

Independence
Dependence
Spiritual Accountability
Organizational Accountability

Some Resource Materials

Books

ACMC, Building Global Vision: 6 Steps to Discovering God's Mission Vision for Your Church (Ft. Wayne, IN: ACMC), 1996.

Borthwick, Paul. *How to Be a World-Class Christian* (Colorado Springs: Victor Books), 1993.

Johnstone, Patrick. *The Church is Bigger than you Think* (Pasadena: William Carey Publishers), 1998.

Johnstone, Patrick and Jason Mandryk. *Operation World,* 21st Century Edition (Atlanta: Authentic Press), 2005.

Piper, John, *Let the Nations Be Glad* (Grand Rapids: Baker Academic), 2003.

Pirolo, Neil, *Serving as Senders* (San Diego: Emmaus Road), 1991.

Pollard, Mike, *Cultivating a Missions-Active Church* (Peachtree City, GA: ACMC), 1988.

Telford, Tom, *Missions in the 21st Century* (Wheaton: Harold Shaw Publishers), 1988.

Van Engen, Charles, *God's Missionary People* (Grand Rapids: Baker Book House), 1991.

Courses

Perspectives, U.S. Center for World Mission, 1605 E. Elizabeth St., Pasadena, CA 91104 (www.perspectives.com)

Organizations

ACMC (Advancing Churches in Missions Commitment), P.O. Box 5266, Fort Wayne, IN 46895 (www.acmc.gospelcom.net)

Periodicals

Evangelical Missions Quarterly, P.O. Box 794, Wheaton, IL 60189 (www.emqonline.com)

Mission Frontiers, 1605 Elizabeth St., Pasadena, CA 91104 (www.missionfrontiers.org)

Resources on the Internet

Missionary Resource Center (www.missionaryresources.org)

Mission Resource Directory (www.mrd.org)

Missions Resources (www.missionsresources.com)

National Association of Missions Pastors (www.missionspastors.org)

World Christian Resource Directory (www.missionresources.com)